In at the
deep end

In at the deep end

deep end

*First experiences of
university teaching*

Edited by
David Allan

*Innovation in
Higher Education Series*

**Unit for Innovation
in Higher Education**
School of Independent Studies
Lonsdale College
Lancaster University
Lancaster LA1 4YN

*First published in 1996 by the Unit for
Innovation in Higher Education, School of
Independent Studies, Lancaster University,
Lancaster LA1 4YN*

ISBN 0 901800 90 2

*Cover design by Rowland & Hird, Lancaster
Printed in Great Britain by Markprint,
Preston, Lancashire*

Preface by
the Series Editor

By the year 2000 Britain will have transformed its elite universities and colleges into a system of mass higher education. With expansion of student numbers and broadening of access it has become increasingly important to understand life at today's universities and colleges, too frequently presented in outdated stereotypes.

So, we are looking for first-hand accounts of experience at the modern university or college of traditional and modern teaching and assessment methods. We would be interested in accounts of all aspects of these institutions such as issues of race, class, age or gender; success and failure; finance; social life and the problems faced by those combining study with jobs and family responsibilities. Appreciation of these issues is crucial not only for students wishing to make the most of their higher education but also for the success of tutors and other staff in providing it.

If you are already – or about to be – involved in higher education in any way, as a student, professor, lecturer, research worker or other staff, we would like to invite you to consider describing and analysing your experience of today's higher education for publication in this series.

John Wakeford

Acknowledgements

We would like to thank *The Times Higher Education Supplement* for their generous and collaborative support. Through their endorsement of the IHE Series, and their assistance with promotional advertising, we are able to further develop the contributions we are making towards greater understanding of, and improvements to, modern university life.

In particular, we are grateful to Ms Helen Priday, Promotions Director of *The Times Higher*, for her support of the Series and for her recognition of the significance of this development.

John Wakeford

I should like to express my gratitude to a number of individuals who made this collection possible.

John Wakeford conceived the idea and passed it on to me for development and execution. Jane Thompson and Liz Hampson assisted as editors, whilst Linda Cook's expertise translated many-and-varied draft copy into a pleasing final text.

Finally, I thank the contributors, whose collective endeavours made the task of the editor much less onerous than it might have been.

David Allan

Contents

Notes on Contributors

David Allan is Lecturer in Independent Studies and History at Lancaster University

Lou Armour is a postgraduate research student and teaches in the Department of Sociology at Lancaster University.

Jill Bourne teaches in the School of Social and Administrative Studies at University College of Wales, Cardiff

Mike Bramley is a postgraduate research student in Linguistics and Modern Languages at the University College of Ripon and York St John.

Janet Cowper is a postgraduate research student in the Department of Linguistics and Modern Languages at the University College of Ripon and York St John

Kirsti Evans has taught in the Department of Religious Studies at Lancaster University. During 1995/96 she holds the Cosmos Fellowship at the University of Edinburgh

Gwilym Games is a postgraduate research student in the Department of History at Lancaster University and teaches American Colonial history

Martin Gough has studied and taught Philosophy at the universities of Birmingham, Cambridge, Leeds and Nottingham, The Open University and for the Philosophical Society of England

Kate Hill is Lecturer in Historical Studies at the University of Humberside and is working on a PhD at Lancaster University

Dominic Janes is Temporary Lecturer in History and Classics at Lancaster University and has recently submitted a PhD in Late Roman Social History to the University of Cambridge

Andrew Nicholls is completing a PhD in History at the University of Guelph, Ontario and he is currently teaching at Canisius College, Buffalo

David Palmer was, until recently, a Research Fellow of Emmanuel College and lectured in the Department of Earth Sciences, University of Cambridge He is now Lecturer in Mineralogy in the Department of Earth Sciences, The Open University

Chris Stokes is a postgraduate research student in the Centre for Science Studies and Science Policy, Lancaster University

Introduction

David Allan

The chapters in this collection offer, probably for the first time, the personal thoughts of those whose task it is likely to be, at the 'chalk-face' of the academic profession, to carry higher education forward into the twenty-first century.

It is hoped that this selection of insights will reveal something of what it is like to be a new teacher in the university of the present and immediate future; what this might suggest about current trends in higher education; and what subsequent entrants to the teaching profession might most profitably be told by those who go before them. It is for the reader, particularly one contemplating or beginning an academic career, to judge how well this aim has actually been served. Nevertheless, some aspects of the chapters which follow are also such as to lend this volume a further, perhaps unanticipated, coherence. To the extent that these are personal statements, they are by turns reflective, instructive, polemical or subversive, according to the lights of the individual author. But they are all - as policy-makers, institutional managers and senior academic staff would also perhaps do well to note - the work of individuals whose first and formative experiences of university teaching are occurring in the rapidly changing higher educational environment of the present day. For this reason above all, it is perhaps worth asking whether, out of the disparate experiences recorded in these essays, the authors collectively might raise issues or provoke thoughts deserving rather wider consideration.

One of the most striking patterns to emerge here is the prevalence of what, in British higher education at least, would have to be recognised as non-traditional contractual arrangements for those engaging in university teaching for the first time. Gone, on the evidence of these new practitioners, are the days when doctoral students usually devoted several years to pristine scholarship and then, armed with a full-time Lectureship, finally re-entered the classroom. The experiences of working in higher education recounted here are, by contrast, often those of people like Kate Hill, Martin Gough and Andrew Nicholls, tackling substantial teaching duties whilst engaged in postgraduate study; or of teachers, like Dominic Janes and Kirsti Evans, subsisting on short-term contracts. Several, including myself, also have significant prior experience of work outside the Groves of Academe - not always acquired by choice.

All of this may add weight to the call of participants such as Martin Gough for a re-articulation of the separate stereotypes of the postgraduate student and the university teacher - part *Educating Rita*, part *Brideshead Revisited*. It also might argue for a re-thinking of the support, development and career structures currently provided by institutions for those who take front-line responsibility for the delivery of education to students, as Janet Cowper insists. Even so, the contribution of Andrew Nicholls, a Canadian graduate student currently teaching in the United States, also serves as a useful reminder that, as it departs from its own long-established patterns, British higher education actually moves rather closer to the mass education systems of many other Western countries. From this different tradition there may be much for British university teachers and their masters to learn.

Other patterns exist which tend to reinforce, through the re-telling of apparently idiosyncratic personal experiences, a growing sense of educational systems in a phase of radical change. The explicit priority accorded to the quality of the classroom experience provided for students - particularly noticeable in Janet Cowper's contribution as well as in David Palmer's impassioned plea on behalf of future science education - can be interpreted, according to one's prejudices, either as a heartening affirmation of vocational commitment or as a cynical and pragmatic sign of these Quality-Assessed, mission-stated times. But where a proper sense of academic responsibility does survive beneath a rising tide of student numbers and bureaucratic demands, it seems at least possible, on this evidence, that attention will still be given to the quality of teaching not because of external compulsion but because of sincere individual concern for the educational enterprise. If nothing else, these might be grounds for thinking that higher education will be well-served in the next century.

More than this, the evidence gathered here may go some way towards confirming what is now widely recognised, that a high regard for students' learning experiences probably entails a distinctly sceptical approach to certain traditional teaching approaches. It plainly necessitates a preparedness to consider alternative strategies and positions, at least where they seem to be appropriate. Some of the contributors, including Lou Armour and Jill Bourne, choose to discuss the conventional lecture as a staple of the British undergraduate curriculum. But their interests in interactive lecturing and in the preparation of 'scrambled egg on toast' to illustrate a point in theoretical sociology, like David Palmer's innovative uses of computer software in the teaching of crystallography, provide strong hints of serious change afoot even here. A greater number of contributors, meanwhile, prefer to engage with the issues raised by more active and participative learning formats. Yet here the problems as well as the advantages of seminars are candidly admitted by Gwilym Games and Chris Stokes.

Despite these reservations, the essential message of this volume probably remains that passive, single-medium, one-directional learning strategies <u>are</u> increasingly being rejected by new practitioners. By the time that the teachers contributing to this collection reach mid-career and attain positions of influence in the early years of the next century, it is even possible that the present slow revolution in teaching methods will have become the new orthodoxy. How this will affect the experiences not only of students but also of the next generation of staff in higher education - those in a position to produce collections such as this twenty years from now - only time will tell.

A closely-related question also addressed with some urgency by authors new to teaching in the 1990s is that of dealing with a more diverse student body than inherited pedagogical traditions or institutional infrastructures were generally designed to accommodate. Where this is so, it often falls to the individual teacher, often an inexperienced postgraduate or relatively junior member of staff, to make the necessary adjustments. Lecture theatres fill with learners increasingly unacquainted with the prior academic knowledge which a previous generation of teachers took for granted in higher education. Seminars, as Dominic Janes has discovered, contain students not only substantially more mature but also much more experienced than the teacher. In default of new policies and structures, it becomes the unenviable duty of the teacher to mediate between ill-equipped or disoriented student and unyielding tradition, an intercessory role for which, as Janet Cowper again notes, little training or support is offered and which potentially invites opprobrium from both parties.

A further common element emerging from these insights into the 'grass-roots' of contemporary university life is the need for sensitivity to the changing expectations which students bring into the academy. David Palmer's technological wizardry, as much as my own concerns to personalise lecture content and style, are consciously the products of an educational environment in which students increasingly have learning needs that are not well-addressed by conventional academic assumptions. Andrew Nicholls's essay, too, is acutely aware of the new problems at an inter-personal level introduced by growing class sizes on both sides of the Atlantic (though, ironically, this phenomenon is exactly the one which Dominic Janes acknowledges has made possible his current employment). On the evidence presented here, new teachers understand that ways of coping with much larger groups, with reluctant participants, and with a growing number of students lacking academic self-confidence, urgently need to be found. Fortunately, as one contributor puts it, "delving into the strategy-bag" is something that many already appear to be doing on a regular basis. Several had also attended a course on 'Tutoring for Postgraduates' organised by the Unit for Innovation in Higher Education at Lancaster University. But the widely-varying levels of relevant training and institutional support reported by the authors may well lead some readers to suspect that some 'strategy bags' elsewhere around the higher education system are probably still inadequately stocked.

Perhaps more experienced academic readers will also be surprised by the obsessive harping of the contributors upon severely practical, mundane matters. One author implies that a spare projector bulb is now essential equipment for the new teacher. Two others confess that alcohol, on the one hand, and the reliability of an elderly motor vehicle, on the other, have, on occasion, been the most important obstacles to the delivery of punctual, polished teaching. A particularly discordant note which echoes throughout these chapters is sounded in relation to furniture: furniture, an apparently marginal consideration which is, in fact, both essential teaching equipment in most academic subjects and a matter of personal status and cultural significance in the academy at large. To Chris Stokes and Kirsti Evans, the appropriate arrangement of seating at times becomes the chief determinant of atmosphere, the precondition of effective learning, the physical expression of a new educational philosophy. To Dominic Janes, the spartan decor and antiquated furnishing of his temporary office is a piece of cool and effective symbolism, a perpetual reproach, a constant reminder of his tenuous employment and menial status. A senior colleague of my own, elevated to the professorship after more than 20 years, was even recently heard to mutter that, in his experience, it was now easier to acquire a Personal Chair than to procure an office chair. These chapters suggest not only the accuracy but the wider importance of this remark in the university of the 1990s.

Finally, whether by way of unsatisfactory contractual conditions, zealous educational evangelisation or ruminations on furnishings, these personal accounts perhaps will leave the reader with, first and foremost, an indelible impression of the new university teacher increasingly as the victim of an identity-crisis. To an extent, perhaps, this is a function of the increasing diversity of activities and institutions embraced by the beguilingly-familiar term 'higher education'. It is also more particularly, no doubt, a result of the ever-wider range of positions, circumstances and arrangements through which an individual eventually comes to be faced with a room-full of students expecting tuition. Chris Stokes and David Palmer, teaching subjects as unrelated as study skills and earth sciences, and in very different institutions, reflect on the difficult, and sometimes disturbing, encounters of new and junior teachers with the prevailing ideologies and entrenched power structures within their respective departments. Others, however progressive their educational principles, still worry that their tender years, their lack of a formal teaching qualification or recognisable academic post, prevent them from attaining the gravitas, the sheer differentiating authority, that many students patently expect and antique, yet tenacious, traditions apparently still seem to require.

One thing above all, then, is clear about starting to teach in the modern university; one thing which has probably always been true. Status, and its resulting empowerment, still matters both to teacher and to student. Its denial - undoctored, untenured, untrained or, significantly, without respectable office furniture - truly flings the new university teacher 'in at the deep end'.

Entering the Fray

Chris Stokes

I arrive ten minutes early. I might have squeezed in a few more minutes of preparation, but I want to make sure the tables and chairs are properly arranged before the session begins.

Once through the door, I take in the scene. A handful of my students are already here. The tables have been cleared to the margins and the chairs, about twenty-five in number, describe a large circle in the middle. It is too large; we shall only be seven or eight if everyone turns up. Two pairs of early students are sitting on opposite sides. Acres seem to separate them.

I wasn't expecting them to be this early. Should I ask them to help me rearrange the furniture? I deliberate. I decide not to bother them then regret it. But I stick with the decision. Meanwhile, I seem to have walked to the front. I'm sitting down. I have some papers with me, a few notes, some handouts and what not. I shuffle the pages and bore into them with my eyes; it's safer than looking around. I'm a bag of nerves. Ten minutes to go before I can start. What do I do now? What do I do now? What do I do now? That question swells in my mind until there's no space left for an answer.

I lift my leaden head and manage to blurt out a conversation opener to the nearest student, John. "Do you live on campus?" He says "Yes." Just think, if I make a mistake now, if my nerves get the better of me and I say something unexpected, everything could collapse. I say, "What's your room like? Is it as bad as I've heard they are?" It sounds banal, I think, even as

I'm pronouncing the words. But it seems to work. John answers (he quite likes it!). Soon Peter joins in. A conversation of sorts breaks out. I feel my first wave of relief. One down; how many more to go?

This was my introduction to teaching, or rather to tutoring. Officially I'm a group tutor. I'm not the usual sort of tutor though; I don't run tutorials to support a lecture series delivered by a senior member of staff. Instead, I run a weekly series of fifty-minute group sessions for three terms, which together make up the core of a first-year programme in Independent Studies. My students are additionally free to come and see me for individual advice outside the group sessions. Ostensibly, my course is on the information society and information highways. But it is also a vehicle - one among several parallel courses in the department with a variety of ostensible subjects - for conveying research and study skills.

Two things I most certainly am not is a teacher or a lecturer. These terms are more or less dirty words in my department - although, as you'd expect, they do slip out from time to time. No. We don't teach. We tutor or facilitate. In group sessions I sit whilst talking and only get up occasionally to use the blackboard or flip chart or overhead projector. I rarely speak for longer than ten minutes at a stretch. Mostly the students work in sub-groups and I circulate between them, trying to breathe life into moribund or stillborn discussions, trying to corral stray discussions back into the right pen. You know the sort of thing.

As you can see, we're terribly egalitarian.

In the bad old days, teaching was straightforward, I guess. Thomas Gradgrind, the eminently practical man of Dickens's

Hard Times, had only to fill the vessels that were his students with imperial gallons of Facts until they were full to the brim; his only masters and mistresses were Facts and blue books. Teaching nowadays - silly me: I mean tutoring, of course - is an altogether more awkward business, in my department at least. As a tutor I have too many masters and mistresses and they tend to bicker amongst themselves continually.

Take, for example, egalitarianism. In my department this worthy ideal is symbolised by the circle of chairs. That's not to say there is any departmental ordinance insisting on it or special seminar rooms with chairs bolted to the ground in the correct formation; but it is an almost unfailing feature of official gatherings of more than two people, whoever they may be. When I go into the seminar room on my weekly teaching - sorry, tutoring - day, if it has not been interfered with by the unbelievers of some other less forward-looking department, then the tables will be scattered to the four corners and the chairs, like standing stones or toadstools in a fairy ring, will be in a circle. You see, the circle has no asymmetries; it refuses the means whereby a superordinate can physically set itself above its subordinates.

That, I imagine, is the theory, anyway. Unfortunately, the University was built in the late bad old days and its architecture is incorrigibly rectangular. The seminar room where my group session (not lectures, mind) take place is definitely oblong; and at one end there are the usual teaching [sic] paraphernalia: flip chart, blackboard (presumably condemned but still clinging on), and overhead projector.

So that circle of chairs has asymmetry, there is one chair closest to the teaching paraphernalia and to one of the short sides of the room's rectangle. What's more, there is often a gap either side of it noticeably larger than those between the other chairs. Naturally, the students do not dare to sit in it; they reserve it for me. In the last session I have to say I did wonder how they would react if I sat to one side and failed to take the initiative with the usual announcements at the beginning. Perhaps one day I'll try it. In the meantime, I am more equal than others.

But how do I know when to serve equality and when to serve authority? I don't. I just have to play it by ear all the time.

Today, for example, the second of two sub-groups was presenting the fruits of its discussion of a text about the impact of electronic mail and computer conferencing on work. This was the first session in which I had asked students to give presentations standing up and I had asked them to use the overhead projector. Tom, the sub-group's nominated speaker, was standing beside it reading from the screen. Now Tom is not timid, but he found himself competing with two members of the other group who were talking none-too-quietly to one another. He paused, waiting for a break in their talk, but none came. A couple of other students laughed awkwardly.

What do I do? Remember, I'm not a teacher or lecturer but a tutor, a facilitator. I'm a member of the group, almost. On these terms, how can I impose? On the other hand, this could get embarrassing. The two who are talking may not have the sensitivity to stop; Tom may not have the nerve to raise his voice authoritatively. Then again, perhaps I should let it get more embarrassing; that way Tom may be pushed into taking control himself and come away with new self-confidence and respect from his peers. Eventually, I turned in the general direction of the miscreants and asked for "some hush while Tom speaks". They apologised and stopped talking. Tom continued. I felt I had done the right thing. The voice of authority had spoken.

I'm not always so fortunate. In an earlier session I spoke with the voice of authority and regretted it. I was bringing a session to a close (doesn't that make it sound as though everything was under control?). We had been discussing a passage from a well-known neo-Luddite treatise opposed to the 'cult of information'. I asked what the main argument of the passage was. A keen student, Steven, volunteered an answer. I thought he missed the main argument in favour of a subsidiary point. I tried to say so without discouraging him. I was anxious but could see I hadn't upset him too much because he tried a new, slightly different, answer, but still not one I thought correct. Now I was in a very tight spot. I could have taken the line of least resistance and said, "Yes, that's it." If I'd been in one of the coffee bars talking to Steven alone, that's probably just what I would have done. But I didn't feel I could pull it off convincingly in front of the others. I still thought he was wrong. In the event, I said I didn't think that was the main argument either. Steven looked deflated. I hurried onto another track. I was unhappy. I made a mess of the last five minutes.

Tutoring like this may not be Gradgrinding. It may be a step forward, recognising that the learner is not a *tabula rasa* waiting to be written on by the teacher. But there is no escaping from the fact that, however worthy it is, it's more than just the open exchange of ideas to the benefit of all. For one thing, it reinforces a whole set of identities and social relationships: the student as supplicant, inexpert, subordinate, consumer, payer, dependant, wanter of what he or she has not; the tutor (or teacher or lecturer) as expert, superior, supplier, earner, provider of the scarce resources he or she has; the university as emporium, centre of learning; the graduate as employable, deserving, decent; and, inevitably, the graduate of the University of Life as also-ran.

I have a particular difficulty with the way in which the tutor-as-expert tutoring the student-as-inexpert can so easily slip into bolstering academic orthodoxies. In my second group session, we looked at the practice of citation. Working from guidelines prepared within the department (which can be a time-saving godsend to the tutor trying to do a PhD outside the classroom), I asked the students to rank a variegated collection of documents, books, articles and electronic documents from the World Wide Web in order of academic respectability. "Which would you be most happy to cite to defend an argument you may want to make?" I asked. I also handed out style sheets for the MLA and Harvard bibliographic styles.

It wasn't until a later meeting of the ten or so who tutor on these courses (another godsend to inexperienced tutors) that I began to have my doubts. We were running through a workshop that our students would shortly be experiencing. One activity amounted to going through a typical student essay with all the citations removed, marking all the places where we thought there ought to be a citation. I felt some tutors were going overboard (perhaps I should confess to being a former engineer among tutors who mostly graduated in the humanities and social sciences). I began to play Devil's Advocate, asking what the difference was between common, uncitable knowledge and knowledge that 'belonged' to citable authors.

A few days later, I found myself speaking to Tom about his plan for his first substantial piece of work. He had missed the session on citation. I summed it up for him; I was advising him to do a piece of work that would give him practice in some of the skills we had already gone over. But I gave Tom a very different story from the one I gave in the group session. I told him not that this is how things ought to be done; I told him that this is how things are done and how you do things if you want to fit into the cosy world of the academy. I felt like a firebrand. I think I felt rather pleased with myself too.

I remember some of the reasons I had for choosing to take up the job of tutor in this second year of my PhD. There was the money I'd earn to eke out my grant, the extra few lines on my CV, the chance to see what teaching or tutoring is like. But it was two others that clinched it, I believe. For one, I'd be forcing myself to develop a much closer understanding of my subject. Many people have told me that the best way to learn a subject is to have to teach it. For another, as someone interested in the sorts of things said in any setting about information highways and the information society, I thought I'd have access in the shape of the seminar room to a setting I otherwise wouldn't get access to. In other words, I thought I could learn from my students while I tutored them.

The peculiar nature of the course I tutor on has meant that I have not and shall not be forced to develop that much closer understanding of my subject. I must spend more time picking apart the research skills that I formerly took more or less for granted than I do reading all the books I can find on my subject. I'm not sure whether that's a good thing or a bad thing. As for learning from my students, the best is yet to come. With the plans for their first pieces of assessed work now in, I am genuinely looking forward to reading the completed essays, reports, plays. Six weeks into this first term, I'm in two minds, no, more than two, about my decision to tutor. But most of the time I'm glad.

If I had to give advice to prospective tutors, teachers, facilitators, it would be:

1   don't take too much notice of advice; and

2   since expecting the unexpected is very time consuming (there's so much unexpected), it may be worth instead not expecting the expected (especially if it's based on advice).

So you think you're a lecturer now?

Jill Bourne

This chapter takes the form of a diary which I kept before and during my first year as a part-time university lecturer. I had already spent two years tutoring small groups. I had also been on a training course at Lancaster in 1994. But I had never done any formal lecturing and was filled with apprehension and dread at the thought of standing up in front of more than forty students. The diary particularly concentrates upon the thoughts and feelings which emerged prior to, during and after those early lectures.

29 July

I've just finished a course on tutoring in higher education and am beginning to wonder if I've taken on too much in trying to lecture on three courses whilst attempting to complete my PhD. This will, after all, be my final year, or at least the final year of funding, and I should really be concentrating on my own research. But the chance to do some lecturing was too good an opportunity to refuse; it will give me at least another line on the C.V. and, at best, a lot of valuable experience. I've actually always said that I don't want to teach. This should allow me to get a taste of what it would be like to do so, without the commitment of a full-time post. Who knows? I might even find that I enjoy it.

2 August

I've had to prepare a course outline, objectives and lecture programme for all three courses I'm going to teach on. Thanks to a little help from one of my former lecturers, who is about the only one who actually treats me like a colleague, I've managed to get it written. Let's hope it's satisfactory.

20 September

A phone call to the institution today confirms that they <u>are</u> going to employ me; but still no contract has appeared. It's rather a good feeling telling people that I'm a university lecturer - though I do feel a bit of a fraud! Off to the Medical Sociology Conference in York on Friday. The only thing on my mind now is whether I'll be able to present 'the paper' in a coherent fashion - if I'm able to do it at all.

26 September

It was a success. I managed to get through the paper without any major blunders. Now I know that if I can do it in front of more than forty people who know so much more than I do, I can certainly lecture to students who ought to know much less!

28 September

Meeting with a new colleague about room allocation, number of students etc. I'm amazed that she doesn't seem to question my ability, or lack of it, to do the job. I'm beginning to look forward to it.

I've now written the lecture programme, essay titles and the reading list. It took me two hours to write two essay questions. I wish they had gone over that on the course: it would have been really useful. I found it very difficult to word a question which was clear and concise, and which I thought the students would understand. I must also get on with preparing the lectures.

3 October

Enrolment this week: it looks as if the students are coming out of the pavements. My first lecture is next Monday the 10th; only a week to go! How on earth am I going to gear myself up for walking into that room?

The first lecture is almost finished: no-one told me how much time it would take to prepare - more than five hours! (So much for earning thirty pounds an hour; more like six pounds an hour.) Still, I guess that, if I do the same ones next year, they will only need slight revision. Now I can see why lecturers give the same lecture over and over again.

9 October

Tomorrow is the big day. My stomach is churning already: no Sunday lunch for me today. The lecture is all ready, with what I hope are interesting quips. A friend who is a lecturer in a college has told me that the first five minutes are the most crucial: if you don't get their attention for that period then you lose them for the rest of the time. Let's hope I pass muster.

10 October

08.15 Print up lecture, get photocopying done.

10.00 Go for a coffee to calm the nerves. Thank goodness for a supportive friend.

12.00 Pick up the relevant notes, photocopies and acetates. Off I go. Quick trip to the loo first I think!

13.15 It's over. And what a relief that it went well and I actually enjoyed it. One slight problem: even though I'd checked the room, made sure that the OHP was there and working, and that I had enough chalk etc, I hadn't anticipated that it might not be a matter of using chalk at all. The room was in fact set up for pens and a whiteboard. Hence a rushed trip to the secretary to get the necessary equipment. I won't make that mistake again.

The students were a bit quiet and didn't respond much to my attempts to engage them in interaction. It appears that they're not used to that type of teaching in lectures: do I persevere, or just go in and talk for 50 minutes? I think that would bore me, let alone them. They did, after all, seem to respond to personal anecdotes. I'll try doing a bit more of that so that they can see the relevance of what I'm trying to put across.

As they are all women students, I must also make sure that I don't get too hooked up on feminist theories and remember to emphasise the drawbacks of the empirical work that is undertaken by some feminists. It would be so easy to get caught in the trap of blaming it all on men and a capitalist, patriarchal society.

16 October

Here I am again, writing the lecture for tomorrow. I really must try to get more organised.

17 October

09.00 Lecture printed up, acetates and photocopies still to do. Thank goodness the lecture is not until 12.10.

10.00 Panic stations: the photocopier is jammed. I'll have to try to get access to another one. Apparently this is common on a Monday morning.

11.15 Finally done all the photocopying.

12.00 Here we go again.

13.15 I enjoyed that. They seemed to be a bit more responsive today. I guess that they have to get used to my style of teaching. Now I know why one of my A-level teachers used to be so understandable. He used to relate what he was telling us to everyday life. I find myself doing this to a small degree: is this because it's what I found to be the easiest to understand? It certainly helped when I was faced with a sea of blank faces whilst trying to explain theoretical sociological perspectives on the family. Talk about having to think on your feet! Still, at least I recognised that they were having problems and tackled the subject from a different angle. I guess that this is what is known as 'interactive teaching'.

I've promised to do the students a handout of a potted version of the different theoretical perspectives for next time; but how on earth do I explain Phenomenology to them? They seem to like having handouts. How was it that John (the training course leader) described them? Something to do with 'take-home tangibles'?

24 October

Another lecture written the night before. Perhaps that's the way I work best. Some might call it 'time management'; others would say that I'm not very organised. But so long as I have it done in time, there's no real problem. At least it's fresh in my mind when I go into the class.

The second theory lecture today. The handouts helped and the students appeared to be following the concepts. One actually asked for clarification which I felt was encouraging: at least they are awake! I'm looking forward to next week when we start to look at the more empirical data.

31 October

The Family, Work and Leisure today. I'm surprised at the number who said that they wanted to stay at home after having a baby. They seem to be more responsive now, asking and answering questions, which is much better than me just standing there lecturing at them. But I felt as if I was losing it at times today; I couldn't seem to concentrate.

5 November

Now I know what was wrong last week: I was going down with the 'flu. I just made it home before collapsing into bed where I've spent the last five days. I don't think I've got enough energy to write this lecture for tomorrow, let alone give it.

7 November

There is one girl who just stares right through me, really putting me off. What can I do? I've tried nodding and smiling towards her, but so far there's been no reaction. Is it me or is she like this in all of the classes? I decided to be 'up front' and tell them I've been ill. They were actually very sympathetic. Perhaps less formal preparation is better.

Today was quite lively. Perhaps talking about food and mealtimes is something these particular students see as being relevant to their degree. John was quite right about teaching having to have some meaning to the students. Maybe I need to ensure that I make the relevance of the topic more obvious. I do refer back to what we have done previously, and make clear the relevance of the topic to the family *per se*. But perhaps I don't explain enough how it relates to the wider course, Family Studies. I must try to do that next week.

14 November

The prepared lecture took a back-seat today. They were so interested in surrogacy that it seemed to dominate; at least, it held their interest. It confirms my earlier view that I need to relax a bit more and not be quite so formal with the presentation. I'm amazed at how much I'm able to recall from memory. I'm certainly much better at thinking on my feet, reacting to the issues they raise which are relevant to the topic, than at delivering a lecture as if it were a formal paper presentation. I think I'll make it slightly different next week and split them up into groups to discuss the concepts of motherhood and fatherhood. I'll try to find a couple of relevant statements which I can use.

21 November

10.10 Trying the new format today. I'll put them into four groups and get them to discuss statements like 'what is a mother/father?'

13.15 Talk about Sod's Law. Why is it today of all days that I go to photocopy some material while the students are in their discussion groups? And who do I meet but the Head of Department?!

What a reaction! They were still talking about the issues we had raised when they were leaving the room. This is <u>definitely</u> the way to get issues such as these across, even if it's not really very practical for more theoretical aspects of the course. I'll have to work out how to combine the two approaches. The main problem is time: there is just not enough time to fit everything in. I never realised that fifty minutes could go so quickly. And there I was at the beginning of the course panicking that I would not have enough to say!

28 November

10.00 Their essays are due in today. I've already had three come to see me for extensions. I guess I'll be able to tell when I mark these whether or not I am doing a 'good job'. The responsibility is enormous. I dread to think what I'll feel like when it comes to their exams.

13.15 One girl said that she had been up since five o'clock trying to finish her essay. Do I come across as that much of a tyrant? I know my own children say that I can look very stern. I do hope that I've not created that impression with the students. It's a difficult business, trying to be approachable but not over-friendly. An isolating existence, life in a classroom. I guess only time and experience will reveal all.

Five important tips for new teachers in higher education:

1   Find out where the nearest lavatory is.

2   Double the time you've already allocated for writing a lecture and marking essays.

3   Get a 'novice' to read through your lecture to ensure that it is understandable to people who know nothing about your subject. (My fifteen-year-old daughter did mine.)

4   Don't worry about missing things out: <u>they</u> won't know you have, and you can always fit it in next time.

5   Most important, be <u>yourself</u>. If you try to hide behind a false persona you will only get caught out.

Good luck!

Evangelising Science in the Nineties:
New Tools for New Times

David Palmer

I began my scientific career as a 'rock hound', collecting minerals, fossils and rocks. Here were natural objects of great beauty and variety. I built up quite a collection of 'stones' (as my parents called them) which soon threatened to crash through the floorboards of my bedroom.

One day, faced with a pretty mineral I couldn't identify, I found a book filled with beautifully illustrated minerals and gems. I was soon able to identify my red stone. But, instead of going back to my collecting, my attention was drawn to other illustrations in the book. In particular, there were pictures showing brightly-coloured spheres arranged in regular patterns, and connected to each other by little sticks. This, I learned, represented part of the crystal structure of my mineral: the underlying arrangement of atoms and chemical bonds. Here was beauty, not on a scale of a centimetre, but ten million times smaller: an unseen world of geometric patterns. Beauty led from the visible, through to the unseen world of crystal structures and their atomic arrangements.

Years later I was preparing for my first mineralogy lecture. I had taken over a colleague's course at rather short notice and I was trying to find a way of enlivening what was generally regarded as a solid, but dull course. The problem was that the teaching tended to get bogged-down in details of crystal structures: the structures described were all very complex and, being three-dimensional, were difficult to visualise. Traditionally, lecturers resorted to schematic diagrams, supplemented by (very dusty) ball-and-stick models.

Unfortunately, this merely emphasised that one couldn't see the wood for the trees; and, for a worryingly-large proportion of students, that was the end of mineralogy.

I thought back to the way that my own interest in the subject had developed. It certainly hadn't come from attending under-graduate lectures on the subject. That had deepened rather than inspired my curiosity. Then I remembered my little mineral collection, and that beautifully-illustrated book. I had become interested in crystal structures because minerals were objects of great beauty; and that beauty was reflected at the scale of atoms and bonds, in the underlying crystal structures.

But how could one convey this very personal aesthetic appreciation to a class full of students? Merely peppering my lectures with pretty pictures would only serve to reinforce the traditional image of minerals in dusty glass cabinets: silent objects to be observed, with respect, at a distance. If that wasn't bad enough, there was still the problem of conveying three-dimensional information. Static, two-dimensional diagrams were no use.

I had already rejected traditional ball-and-stick crystal models as being over-complicated. These models also suffered from being fixed: they couldn't suddenly be transformed into simpler representations. Of course, one could buy additional models - but a pile of separate models on a lab bench creates more clutter and confusion than is worthwhile.

I decided to replace traditional props and the blackboard with a computer. My aim was to provide a sense of interactivity - of learning as a two-way process. A static view of a model conveys certain information to the user; but I wanted the user directly to control the model: to rotate; to specify which part of the structure to plot; to 'zap' away particular atoms; to measure distances or angles, and so forth. I wanted to create a 'real-time' experience that was also aesthetically pleasing. I might have used existing software, but this was vastly expensive and only ran on over-priced, 'user-hostile' computer workstations. I needed powerful software, but it had to run on inexpensive computers and, most importantly, provide a 'user-friendly' interface that would appeal to untrained students.

A few years earlier I had started writing a computer program to draw crystal structures. This was written as much out of desperation with existing software as for any other reason. I'd needed to plot the positions of atoms in a crystal I was studying and there was nothing else suitable. Maybe I could develop this as a tool for self-guided exploration and for presentation in lectures?

I ended up with a computer program called *CrystalMaker*: a tool to explore and manipulate crystal structures. Atoms and their chemical bonds could be represented as traditional 'ball-and-stick' models (albeit brightly-coloured and dust-free), and these could be rotated in real-time by dragging the computer mouse across the screen. I added photo-realistic shading to make models look three-dimensional. But, unlike 'real' models, this computer model could be entirely transformed by the user. With just a click of the mouse button the crystal could be redrawn: hiding the confusing chemical bonds, leaving just the atoms themselves, scaled so as to indicate their correct sizes. At another click, clusters of atoms could be replaced by simple polyhedral shapes, and so on. I gradually added other enhancements to the interactivity, for example allowing students to 'fly through' their crystals and investigate the structure en-route, or to 'lasso' bits of the structure for a closer look.

The next problem was how actually to use the program in my teaching. Fortunately, my department was about to face a Funding Council teaching assessment, and was therefore inclined to spend money on computer equipment. I persuaded them to buy a computer projection panel: an elegant device which can be connected to a computer and placed over an overhead projector. For classroom use I chose the most powerful and user-friendly personal computers - *Power Macintosh*. Thus armed, I began my course.

The first lecture began with a rotating crystal structure projected on the front wall of the lecture theatre. I was able to switch from writing on an overhead projector to picking up a crystal on the computer, zooming in and flying onto the objects of interest. I used my program, and Apple's wonderful *QuickTime* software, to make short movies of mineral behaviour: animating the changes in crystal structures that happen with changing temperature or under pressure in the Earth's interior.

I was particularly keen that students should use the software themselves for self-guided exploration and discovery. In our practical classes we laid out a number of computers next to traditional crystal models. Being able to duplicate a model on the computer and then to transform its appearance in order to simplify it: this was very satisfying. I eventually had difficulty persuading people to leave the computers and return to the main paper-and-pen exercises!

Using new technology in a live situation is, of course, inherently risky; and one has to be well-prepared. This was made very apparent to me one morning when, due to a misunderstanding with the support staff, I arrived at a lecture to find my computer, projection panel, overhead projector and assorted cables, all neatly arranged at the front - but with nothing connected. After ten minutes of frantic spaghetti-sifting, I suddenly realised that there weren't enough power sockets to fire up the system. It wasn't quite the dramatic entrance I'd planned!

Initial reaction from my colleagues was mixed. Some were genuinely excited and very encouraging throughout the project. Others were more sceptical, apparently fearful of the dangers of "trivialising science". It is encouraging for me to see that, having developed new tools and approaches to teaching, colleagues are gradually introducing them into their own courses.

Whilst I found my own teaching very rewarding at a personal level, one has to say that, under the current academic regime, taking time and effort to promote science education is more likely to harm than to enhance one's long-term career opportunities. The rewards for developing innovative teaching are far fewer than the prizes and accolades given to research workers. The present system of incentives conspires against innovation in education precisely because it places undue reliance on the opinions of a research elite who are largely insulated from the problems of teaching science in an increasingly sceptical decade. What I have come to find particularly unacceptable is the view that university teaching is a necessary evil: students are merely 'bums on seats', blank tokens to be processed in exchange for government funding of research.

One hopes that the recently-implemented teaching assessments of university departments will eventually have as much 'bite' as university research reviews. In the long term, as universities become more market oriented, this must surely be the case. But, in the short term, I am not so sure.

It is now, more than ever before, that we need a public which is informed about the technological revolution transforming our world. But the impact of television - and more recently the multi-media revolution - has meant that young people now expect slick, high-quality presentations delivered with authority and conviction. The old stereotypes of bumbling white-coated bespectacled scientists in their ivory towers simply have to go. We need to escape from the treadmill of research ratings and preach a new educational gospel that is vibrant and exciting. We must evangelise science.

Key points:

1 **Be sure of the message you want to communicate to your students.**

2 **Don't feel constrained by existing, conventional course materials: look around for new ideas and better tools.**

3 **Computer animation can be a very effective way for students to understand complex phenomena - but keep the computer interface as simple as possible.**

4 **Recognise that whilst computers are excellent for certain things, they are not best for everything!**

5 **Don't underestimate the importance of 'play learning' for students: let them explore for themselves, to reach their own, individual understandings.**

6 **You may be computer literate, and well-prepared; don't assume your colleagues are so well prepared (or understanding).**

7 Don't expect your department to offer any special recognition or career advancement to you for your innovative teaching. However, your reward will probably come from seeing students enjoying learning.

Postgraduate tutoring: an education for all

Janet Cowper

Rather than indulge in a long diatribe about how I survived as a postgraduate tutor with no previous experience of tutoring, in an institution which had no previous experience of postgraduate tutors, I would like simply to provide a list of things which I think universities should know about postgraduate tutors, together with a complementary list of points which I believe postgraduates should, in their turn, know about teaching. It is to be hoped that this might contribute to heightening awareness of the problems (and the potential) associated with postgraduate tutoring, which, in a sense, can certainly be an education for all concerned.

The points made here have been drawn from my own brief experience of postgraduate tutoring (only eight weeks at the time of writing), and from informal comments from other postgraduates, lecturers, and participants in a training course held at Lancaster in 1995. For the sake of clarity, and to reflect the dual purpose of this chapter, the points have been divided into: 'five things that universities should know about postgraduate tutors' and, since it is only fair, 'five things that postgraduates should know about postgraduate tutoring'.

Five things that universities should know about. postgraduate tutors

1 *Postgraduates take teaching seriously*

Postgraduates are usually those who have benefited from, and so are most likely to appreciate, high quality teaching. Many postgraduates are determined to draw upon their (recent) experience of learning to address the needs of students in a way which is both effective and sympathetic. Furthermore, all the postgraduates who I have talked to have shared a 'professional' commitment to teaching: many intend subsequently to enter teaching-related professions. This level of commitment is reflected in the amount of time postgraduate tutors may take over preparation (one, for example, spent ten hours preparing for a one-hour seminar); but also in the amount of stress experienced as part of the process of teaching. A 'professional' attitude is particularly evident in the surprise many express when they find that formal training is not always the norm for university teachers, and that it is definitely not the norm for new postgraduate tutors.

2   Teaching experience feeds back into postgraduate work

Inevitably, experience of teaching will feed back into all areas of a postgraduate's life, including their research and dissertation work. Moreover, the increased academic confidence and communication skills acquired through successful teaching experience will be significant personal gains for any postgraduate tutor. Unsatisfactory experience of teaching, however, can conversely sap the postgraduate's morale, self-esteem and confidence to do anything at all.

3   Postgraduate tutors need help

Many postgraduate tutors, especially those in their first year, are afraid to ask for help or advice about teaching. Many have the impression that they are expected already to have the presentation skills and subject knowledge to teach effectively. Most find that presenting material as a tutor is very different from approaching it as an undergraduate. Lack of confidence often prevents the postgraduate tutor from seeking advice.

They may also feel that their difficulties and confusion will be construed as weakness, or perhaps that their problems will seem trivial to experienced teaching staff. Moreover, postgraduate tutors may not even know who to approach or where to look for information. Resource rooms might exist, but the postgraduate may not know about them; or they may not contain information relevant to their situation. Many things which postgraduate tutors need help with are very basic: how to get the visual and other aids they may need (OHPS etc), what to do if a student asks for an extension, what to do if a room has been double booked etc. Other problems may be more complicated and personal: what to do if you 'foul up' in a seminar, how to handle a difficult student or group, how to cope with impromptu tutorials, and so forth.

4   *Postgraduates need a clear division between research and teaching*

Several postgraduate tutors that I've met seemed to resent time in research tutorials being taken up with discussions about teaching. Whilst those discussions are of course important, many postgraduates feel that they should be separate from research. This problem is of course accentuated when the postgraduate's study-advisor or supervisor is actively involved in the same teaching programme.

5   *Postgraduates like to teach*

Most postgraduate tutors welcome the break that teaching gives from research. All express a sense of achievement when sessions went well. Most clearly enjoy the interaction with undergraduate students and, whenever possible, with other members of the teaching team. Several say that they felt much more a part of the department since they began tutoring. In short, tutoring can be, and often is, a very positive experience for the tutor.

Five things that postgraduates should know about teaching

1 *Teaching can take up a lot of time*

Contact time is the minimum time spent teaching. Preparation for a seminar or lecture takes hours, sometimes even days; marking and tutorials take up yet more time. Several postgraduate tutors have realised that the worst aspect of teaching is the conflict which they feel between the time they need to devote to research and the time required for teaching.

2 *Don't expect confidence to improve immediately (if ever)*

Even experienced lecturers experience 'stage-fright' and nervousness when teaching, especially when they are taking a group they have never taught before. It is best to accept this nervousness and stress as integral to teaching. It is symptomatic of the 'professional' commitment you are making. Breathing exercises and relaxation techniques can help, and, of course, thorough preparation can go a long way to reducing the stress of teaching.

3 *Advice and help is available if you ask for it*

Most postgraduate tutors (myself included) feel reluctant to ask for help or advice. However, many people are more than willing to offer advice if you ask. Try to make their job easier by identifying problems and listing questions to ask. Talk informally to other lecturers: they are usually quite happy to tell you about their experiences and their methods of work.

4   *Sometimes you have to prepare yourself for teaching*

Some institutions do not have a formal policy of teacher training. However, whilst I believe that it is extremely important that this deficiency is addressed, there are several ways in which any tutor can prepare for teaching:

a) Ask to observe lecturers (pick a good one). Sit in on a full lecture or part of one. Watch what the lecturer does, and watch the class's reaction. Always make a list of points to take away. Sometimes lecturers even appreciate feedback about their teaching methods and performance.
b) Offer to do presentations - perhaps in your research area - so as to get used to preparing and delivering material to an audience.
c) Read about workshops and teaching techniques (though this is no substitute for 'hands-on' experience). All university libraries have information on teaching.
d) Joint an amateur dramatics group!!! I'm not joking: one way of overcoming the fear of performing in front of groups is simply to <u>do</u> it.

5   *Postgraduate tutoring can be fun*

Nearly everyone said that, on the whole, they <u>enjoyed</u> teaching and found it <u>stimulating</u>. Several postgraduates said they welcomed the opportunity to try out new academic ideas. Some said that if they kept the sessions reasonably informal, the students' enjoyment was infectious.

These are only some of the many points that are relevant to postgraduate tutoring. I am sure that every tutor, and every institution which uses tutors, could think of many other things that each should know about the nature of postgraduate tutoring. However, the main advice that I'd like to offer, which also serves as a conclusion, is this:

Always keep your institution informed about your experience

The only way to change attitudes, for institutions to learn about postgraduate tutors and to address their particular problems, is for postgraduates and institutions to communicate. Write short reports (to the student newspaper perhaps); talk to your colleagues; press for some sort of training if this is what you need; and don't be afraid to put forward new ideas.

If all these points are considered, postgraduate tutoring can be a learning experience both for tutors and for the institution they work in. It can be an effective way of meeting student needs. It can bridge the divisions between the postgraduate community, undergraduates and teaching staff. In short, if approached positively and sensitively, postgraduate tutoring can be an education for all.

Avoiding the Greek Chorus:
some thoughts on undergraduate seminars

Andrew Nicholls

In one of his lesser known cases, Sherlock Holmes was able to solve a mystery surrounding a stolen Greek examination, partly because of the personal information a college tutor furnished about the three undergraduates whom he supervised. Ah, for the halcyon days when that kind of acquaintance with one's students was possible! Whereas Mr Soames, the tutor in *The Adventure of the Three Students*, was able to tell Holmes about his pupils' backgrounds, talents, and academic performances, most course instructors and tutorial leaders of today have only the slightest knowledge of the twenty, thirty, or more individuals who fall under their supervision in a given class or seminar. Most of us may be fortunate in not requiring greater familiarity in order to catch cheaters or to solve crimes. But the contrast between our class sizes, and those which apparently existed in Mr Soames' day, is striking for other reasons.

First, it serves as yet another reminder of how large and impersonal our institutions of higher learning - on both sides of the Atlantic - have become. Second, it illustrates how the efforts of faculty and staff have had to be refocussed so as to incorporate greater and greater numbers of students: the result is a general lack of intimacy and familiarity on campus. Finally, it reminds us that the university experience was once expected to entail the exploration of one's subject in conjunction with one's professors, tutors, and fellow students. Times have clearly changed. The undergraduate of today is commonly given the lonely task of processing information and regurgitating it in mass examinations, rather than of learning and developing through the communal give-and-take which was possible in simpler times.

In those situations where there still remains a possibility of establishing rapport and encouraging group participation, the instructor needs to pay even greater attention to developing the right atmosphere in the classroom. This is especially true in undergraduate seminars, where students are given the opportunity to discuss course material; and where the assessment of their performance is based on their verbal contributions. As straightforward as this should be, students are often intimidated by the prospect of speaking at all, let alone of expressing an opinion which they fear will be incorrect, or, even worse, unpopular. The undesirable result can be a room filled with silence: a veritable Greek Chorus of faces which don't speak and which positively refuse to become central players in the drama.

Fortunately, however, the seminar leader can still play an important role in encouraging each student to participate freely and openly, without fear of ridicule or reproach. With adequate planning and forethought, the seminar can be conducted in a manner which elicits regular and meaningful contributions from all members of the class. Too often, as an undergraduate and as a graduate student, I have seen seminar leaders assume a posture which actively discourages discussion and input. I have never forgotten my first undergraduate seminar, in which the teaching assistant informed us that she would not be bothering to learn our names because she would be leaving at Christmas to complete her doctoral dissertation in Brazil. She never explained to us how this prevented her from learning our names. Nor did she say why the prospect of a few months south of the Equator could possibly dampen her enthusiasm for "An Introduction to

Canadian Political Science." (Surely she wouldn't have the chance to probe the intricacies of Canadian Federal-Provincial Relations on the beaches of Rio?) She also used our first meeting to warn us that our essays would receive very harsh treatment if we used any split infinitives - her own pet grammatical peeve.

All of this left an indelible impression with me concerning how a seminar should not be conducted. It was a particularly frustrating experience because the course instructor was otherwise a most stimulating lecturer, one whose style encouraged extra reading and contemplation. Needless to say, however, our enthusiasm for the seminar, and for attending classes given by this individual, had been effectively dampened from the outset. And the tutorial component of this course duly turned out to be a poor contrast with the other four courses I took in my first year.

It has been my view ever since that even the most seasoned seminar leader needs to evaluate his or her handling of tutorials on a regular basis, with a particular eye to encouraging maximum participation. Seminars allow for discussion of course content. But the leader must particularly avoid expecting identical reactions from all students to course material, or uniform quality of contribution. Seminars, after all, are transient groupings of individuals. Each one will take on a life and character of its own. It is therefore imperative that the leader not enter a seminar situation with preconceived notions of how the students will react or perform. Further, because seminar leaders are often graduate students who are eager to flaunt their own recently-acquired knowledge of a given subject, they can have a tendency to try to dominate the discussion, or to offer complicated views on the material, without allowing sufficient time for individual students to demonstrate their own level of understanding. Even if unintentionally, a seminar leader can create an intimidating atmosphere simply by trying to fill 'dead air' with a display of his or her own knowledge. Fortunately, creating an environment which is comfortable for the students, which is conducive to discussion and which encourages students themselves to take centre stage, is relatively easy, provided that the seminar leader adopts a few common-sense practices.

First and foremost, it is essential to be yourself. If you are normally quiet and unassuming, there is no need to try to become a clone of John Cleese in order to put your class at ease. Seminars should be fun as well as informative. But if you prefer to prepare subjects for discussion in advance, and stick to an agenda, then your students will adapt. If you are comfortable with a more spontaneous approach, then by all means apply it. The point is to give them a sense as quickly as possible that you expect their readings or assignments to be completed prior to the seminar, and that they can expect a consistent atmosphere during the class. They also need to understand - as is now commonly the case in Canada - that they will be graded on their participation, and that this is not to be confused with mere attendance.

Because of this, there will be a certain amount of onus on them to become involved. In encouraging involvement, there is no substitute for learning the names of your students as soon as possible. This is particularly crucial in institutions which work on the semester system, where seminar groups might only meet nine or ten times. During the first couple of seminar meetings I always have my students tell me their names when they answer a question, and I make it a personal goal to memorise all of their names by the fourth week of term. I know that students appreciate this effort to create familiarity, as it has constantly been mentioned as a positive practice in my course evaluations. Nothing gives a student confidence like being called by name. And this in turn helps them learn each other's names, which can be an even greater boon for discussions and debates.

When conducting a seminar, I also generally prefer to spend the first few minutes of the class on basic questions of fact. This has the double advantage of revealing whether people have actually done their readings for the week (don't hesitate to call on individuals to provide answers to these initial questions), and also allows you to determine the students' level of comprehension. When students have prepared for class, the opportunity to answer a few basic questions, and to demonstrate their general knowledge, can be a useful stage in getting them to answer more abstract questions or to offer an opinion on a particular subject. The results can be very rewarding, as even the most retiring and shy student, perhaps bolstered by his or her success in identifying Torquemada, may then go on to say a few kind words about the Spanish Inquisition. This in turn should elicit a response from other members of the class, - *et voila*, you have a discussion on your hands!

Another factor which must be considered when conducting a seminar is how to handle those enthusiastic students who are anything but reluctant to participate. This can be a delicate matter. You will not want to discourage them from participating (indeed they may be your most dependable members of the group). But you also need to prevent them from dominating discussions and discouraging others. Here, it may be useful to assess this issue in terms of the length of your course. If a seminar is running for ten weeks, and one or two students seem to dominate in the first week or two, then this can be used to the class's advantage. It will show the more reluctant members that they need not fear your reactions or criticisms and that the atmosphere of your class is in fact conducive to participation. It may also set a standard in terms of the work which is needed to make meaningful contributions to discussions. At the same time, however, the seminar leader should not permit one or two students to dominate, and it may be necessary explicitly to draw others into discussion because... "X should not have to do all the work." Where a particularly voluble individual makes it difficult for others to participate, I have found that it can help to have a private word, outside the class, with that individual. In these circumstances, you can more easily compliment them on their efforts while also pointing out the need to allow others a chance to talk.

Finally, grading students' participation in class can be one of the most difficult aspects of the leader's job. But sometimes, concern over one's own method of grading can actually work against the success of a seminar. I have seen seminar leaders, for example, make scrupulous attempts to note the occasion and quality of every student's contribution to a discussion, yet only create trouble for themselves. Seminars are not golf games, where every stroke needs to be recorded. Indeed, trying to 'keep score' in a seminar can distract the leader from effectively guiding and assessing discussion. This can cause the students to become overly preoccupied with the mark a given answer will earn. I therefore find it preferable to leave grading until the end of the term. If you have learned your students' names and have made an effort to encourage everyone to participate, it should not be difficult to decide upon relative contributions. My preference has in any case always been to develop a sense of the students' overall performances, and not to allow one particularly good or bad day to skew a mark. Others may wish to keep a more specific record of contributions, and the utility of this is not to be underestimated. If you feel the need to do this, it may be better to record observations of the group after the class has ended, so that the act of marking does not inhibit participation and attention.

It can be said then, that encouraging seminar participation requires some initial planning on your part but is even more dependent upon your handling of given situations and duties whilst in class. In the final analysis, there is no hard and fast formula which can guarantee a successful seminar - although sincerity, common sense, and an obvious interest in your students and their views are probably essential. If these basic qualities are present from the outset, the members of your group will be more comfortable when speaking, and the seminar will have a better chance of functioning as it should. As the leader, you will soon find yourself in the challenging position of moderating stimulating discussions among keen participants rather than trying to coax the merest peep from a mute Greek Chorus.

Talking the Tightrope

David Allan

I prepared meticulously for my first lecture.

In my mind I knew exactly the kind of performance I wanted to give: like the one where the lecturer's emphatic gesturing had first signalled the excitement of the specialism I later chose to pursue; or the time when another lecturer, the consummate practical joker, had beguiled us into writing down the previous evening's football results instead of a list of dates and battles. Fond memories such as these provided powerful but inchoate inspiration.

I still faced a serious problem, however. I had had absolutely no relevant instruction or first-hand experience to prepare me for the exercise.

I had a vague idea of what I needed to do. I knew that I probably ought to use overhead transparencies to break-up the lecture into smaller, more digestible chunks. I knew about using striking visual images and memorable anecdotes to get the key points across. I also wanted to see if a joke or a personal aside might be fitted-in so as to make the experience less antiseptic, less dispassionate for both my audience and myself. These, at least, seemed useful intentions with which to work. But I lacked formal guidance or supervision.

Left to my own devices, I realised very quickly that a strategy of intensive planning would be required. In particular, this entailed actually writing out my prepared text in full. It wasn't that I intended literally to read my notes out, word-for-word. It was more that, worried by the possibility of 'drying-up' under the nervous exposure of my situation, I wanted to have something to fall back on in an emergency. That meant having suitable words available in front of me for delivery *verbatim* if necessary.

To this end, I even went to the lengths of marking-up my lecture notes in bold ink in the margins:

HALF-WAY!

Map 4

"......and that's perhaps the most surprising thing about the Thirty Years' War: that Europe managed to get all the way from the compromises in the 1550s to the outbreak of the war in 1618 without any other major international war of religion breaking out in Central Europe.

The state of Europe in 1618 is worth a closer look, because, as you can see on the overhead, ..."

This was to remind me, in case I lost my bearings, where I ought to be starting to put another transparency on the projector and to tell me how far through the lecture I was and how far there was still to go. I also hit upon the ruse (no-one had told me) of building into my notes some optional material, bracketed in red ink. I could introduce or skip this, depending on whether there turned out to be time. (I was aware of the awful possibility of either finishing ten minutes too soon, or, even worse, having to miss out the crucial summary at the end, through misjudgements of timing.) Naturally, in the spirit of detailed preparation, I even had a full dry-run, in front of a mirror, reading out my lecture to myself, just to make sure that I had 50-minutes' worth in my hands. (In retrospect, of course, I feel far more sheepish about having performed to myself in front of a mirror than I ever felt embarrassed in front of a real audience.)

Thus, in terms of my actual delivery, I was eventually as well prepared as it was possible to be. Perhaps even over-prepared. But at least - and this helped allay some of my own nervous anticipation - I felt that I'd planned in such a way as to maximise my chances of delivering a coherent, seamless, varied, personalised and punctual lecture, with some alternatives and room-for-manoeuvre built into my schedule.

A further decision I also took at this first stage of my lecturing career was that my material - my own notes, together with overhead slides and material for circulation to the students - would all be prepared on a word-processor and stored on disk. As well as the much greater security this affords to material into which you'll probably have poured, for a full course, hundreds of hours of your extremely valuable time, there's a second, more tangible advantage. This is, of course, that word-processed materials can very easily be up-dated. Have you ever seen your senior colleagues' lecture notes, dog-eared and illegibly annotated, presumably up-dated piece-meal over the years but increasingly confusing to work from as the marginalia and insertions accumulate? Preparation on disk allows you neatly to chop and change, to scissors-and-paste, to move material around to create new lectures from existing material and to insert existing bibliographies. All in all, it's a labour-saving measure that, I promise you, turns out to be well worth the self-discipline involved in typing it all in the first place.

Other essentially mechanical preparations of this kind, and which I used before that first lecture, would certainly include checking out your venue in advance. This isn't always possible (especially if, as in the case of my own second performance, the lecture involves a guest appearance at a different institution). But either by visiting beforehand or by quizzing your intended hosts, knowing where the lecture is to be given will offer the practical benefit of familiarising you with the layout and equipment, as well as the psychological benefit - not to be discounted - of further reducing the number of uncontrollable imponderables (eg. "But will the room be big enough!?") which can make nervous people, like first-time lecturers, fret even more agitatedly.

Further to reduce the risk of problems coming to light only when you're in front of a baying audience, you should certainly make sure, as I did on that first occasion, that the overhead projector/slide/sound systems are functioning properly and that you know how to operate them. It's clearly better to ask a porter to show you how to control the lights, the blinds or any other fixture before you need to display your new-found dexterity to 200 students. I can well remember being lectured by someone who clearly hadn't done this. He made a complete fool of himself by scrabbling around helplessly looking for the elusive controls to the slide projector:

> "Ah... ... Yes ..... Here it is ....I think I've got it .... Is anything coming on? .... Oh dear .... Hmmm .... Anything yet? .... Yes? .... No .... I can't seem to get it on .... I wonder if someone could go and fetch the porter?"

It's even a fact that some untrusting individuals carry round a spare overhead projector bulb with them, just in case the lamp happens to have exploded during the previous class in the room. Whether I'd actually want to go that far is another matter: it looks like a classic case of academic paranoia. But, once again, the calming psychological effects of having effectively ruled out one more potential disaster by shrewd advanced planning may be reassuring to the novice.

One final aspect of practical preparation which I've found useful right from the outset is particularly worth highlighting. And that's the assessment of your audience. Because they will vary, possibly considerably. My second public appearance, for example, was less than satisfactory in this respect, since my hosts failed to warn me, and I neglected to inquire, about the composition of my audience. If you ever have the misfortune to prepare a nuggety 50-minute lecture on seventeenth-century philosophy for what you presume will be a small professional academic gathering and then turn up to find that your 200 listeners are in fact, to a man and woman, local farmers with distinctly less esoteric interests, you'll be much more careful subsequently in finding out about your audiences in advance. One elderly gentleman, bathed in a post-lunch alcoholic haze, even began snoring audibly before I was half way through! I now always check religiously on the size as well as the character of the group, as this affects how much of a *rapport* you'll be able to develop with them through your performance. With a smaller group, for example, it's possible to reveal more of yourself:

> "The history of the Balkans is no longer, as it seemed only fifteen years ago, of purely academic interest to West Europeans. When I did my O-levels in 1980 I had to learn where

to place Bosnia-Herzegovina, Montenegro and Serbia on the map. At the time it seemed pretty irrelevant; an archaism with no modern significance beyond a minor landmark on the road to an otherwise inevitable First World War. The creation of Yugoslavia seemed to have swept all of that away. I took it for granted that Yugoslavia had a real existence. They were in the Eurovision Song Contest. People went on holiday there. In fact, several of my student contemporaries went off Inter-Railing around Yugoslavia, and came back with nothing more serious than a fierce suntan and a lot of tall stories...."

On the whole, though, familiarity and personal glimpses of this kind tend to work much better with an intimate group of 20 people than with the serried ranks of 200 or so. Only real comic geniuses like Billy Connolly and Ben Elton should probably attempt this most dangerous of tightrope tricks: self-revelation to the masses.

It's also well-nigh essential to understand the specifically academic background of your audience: How much will they know already? Which related courses have they all (or some of them) attended? What's the spread of ability and experience here? And what can I reasonably take for granted? The answers to such questions will particularly influence your presentational strategy in preparing your lecture. An audience largely unfamiliar with your subject may need almost everything explaining to them, often at lengths which, outside the context of an oral lecture, would seem overly pedantic. With such an audience, some concise parenthetic definitions from you, together with regular emphatic recapitulations, are probably a necessity. For example:

> "One of the most significant influences acting on sixteenth-century French political thinkers, like Montaigne who we've just looked at, was the recovery by contemporary scholars and publishers of the writings of ancient scepticism. (Scepticism was a philosophy popular in classical Greece. It stressed the narrow limits of what we know or can know. Sceptics argued that it was stupid to believe that which cannot be proven.) In sixteenth-century France, scepticism of this kind provided for individuals like Montaigne persuasive arguments against belief in any political or religious dogma which could not strictly be shown to be true....."

At the same time, your judgement of the audience's background will also influence how sophisticated and complex you wish to make your treatment of the subject. (One of the sobering discoveries of my early PhD career was that the issues were so much more complicated than the preceding undergraduate course had appeared to suggest: when challenged on this, my former tutor simply shrugged his shoulders apologetically and explained that that had been the "easy-peasy lecture version"). It's actually difficult, and probably unwise, to be too subtle or 'clever' in your arguments when lecturing. On the whole, a typical undergraduate audience in a lecture theatre will benefit most from a reasonably straightforward presentation of a topic and its principal issues of contention. Using an oral presentation to try out an advanced form of critical deconstruction on a difficult text for an audience unfamiliar with either is, I suspect, a recipe for misunderstanding. Tightrope gymnastics of this kind are best confined to the textbook, where the reader will have the opportunity to re-visit them as many times as necessary.

The character of the audience is also, of course, likely to determine how much you'll want to leaven your explanations with amusing digressions and vivid illustrations. Generally speaking, the less expert the audience, the greater your need to rely on regular overhead slides, music, jokes, demonstrations and other diversionary tactics to keep attracting their attention, to keep them amused and to get your points across.

My own early experiences, and the kernel of my advice to others, therefore emphasise the simple virtue of thorough preparation. There is, however, a final point to consider. One thing can't be prepared for in advance of your first performance, and will come, to a greater or a lesser degree, only once you start lecturing. It's that extra special ingredient, the thing which made certain lectures in my own undergraduate years such memorable and inspirational experiences. Quite what it is called is difficult to say. Like the taste of bananas, it's remarkably hard to describe but you tend to know it immediately when you encounter it. Perhaps it's simply a matter of *personality* or *charisma*. That's something which, sadly, no amount of preparation, no training literature and no staff development course is going to pump into you. But, engaging with an audience, interesting them in what you are saying and encouraging them to go out to work on it themselves, is probably, I suspect, as important as having a full set of notes or carrying round a spare projector lamp.

Key points:

1 Plan your lecture thoroughly, with good notes and appropriate materials.

2 Check the venue and any facilities which you intend to use.

3 Know your audience: its size and composition, the motivation and academic background of its members.

4 Don't under-estimate how difficult it may be for them to grasp, perhaps for the first time, complex ideas and arguments delivered orally; in other words, keep things simple.

5 Remember, finally, that some anxiety on your part is a good thing: lecturing is a performance art and a nervous edge will give you the adrenalin 'buzz' to perform to your potential.

My first seminars

Kate Hill

Being asked to teach students, while still basically a student yourself, puts you in a rather strange position. Don't misunderstand me. It's incredibly useful, rewarding, and so forth, as an experience. But for me (and I imagine this to be quite common), the weeks before my first seminars saw me in a state of growing terror that I did not possibly have the maturity, knowledge, experience or authority to do this - despite the fact that I didn't think a seminar was actually about any of these things but rather about co-operation and equality of contribution, in effect a mutual learning experience. Indeed, the main problem once I had embarked on teaching was not my perceived lack of authority or knowledge. It was simply how to cope with students who wouldn't do anything unless specifically instructed to.

I now believe, as a result, that there are two main problems to tackle when taking your first seminars. The first is to get yourself sorted out; and the second is actually to make the seminars productive and worthwhile for the students. But these concerns can be in conflict. Certainly, with my beginner's nerves, I needed to feel secure; to sense that things were under control; to know that there was a rigid plan for me to follow. But I also know that that same element of unpredictability and spontaneity is vital to a successful seminar. My appreciation of this latter quality was enhanced when I took the 'Tutoring for Postgraduates' course at Lancaster. But this chapter concerns itself with my considered thoughts on how best to address both of these pressing concerns.

Basically the first five minutes of a class are crucial for your own confidence. I was introduced to the group by a hardened, veteran lecturer, who then watched me stutter, blush and generally 'go to pieces' under his beady eye. In fact, it's much better not to have anyone around at this stage who's going to make you feel more nervous (except the students of course, but you and they are just going to have to get on!). Also, if you're there when the students arrive, they may perhaps mistake you for one of them but it does save you the daunting task of walking into the room with countless pairs of eyes upon you.

As a postgraduate student, not much older than the group I was teaching, my expectations were that I would have no problems creating a relaxed, open atmosphere. I had anticipated that the challenge would in fact be to be taken seriously and to assume the authority necessary to direct and structure the emerging discussion. In fact, the biggest surprise I had was the readiness with which the group handed over initiative and responsibility to me. The seminar consisted of ten to fifteen people, a group large enough for each participant to feel relatively anonymous. This was exacerbated by a fixed seating arrangement which tended to isolate me and allowed them to try to blend into the background. However inexperienced and lacking in leadership qualities you may feel in your own mind, I suspect that, if a large group of students knows you are 'in charge', they will try to force you into doing all the work and taking all the responsibility for the seminar. Allowing this to happen at the outset does not establish a good precedent.

In retrospect, and in order to counteract this undesirable tendency, I should have done something about the seating arrangements - even if it meant ripping tables up or (more realistically) changing rooms. No-one should be more or less conspicuous than anyone else; and that certainly includes you. It also makes sense to force students each to do something at the very start: for instance, have everyone participating in some sort of introduction activity before you introduce yourself and the course. When I got round to an introduction activity, it went really well; people were laughing and, as far as I could tell, really enjoying themselves. It was a revelation! The potential problem, though, is that first years may have already gone through several introduction exercises in the last three days: so try to make yours different!

When I started taking seminars I also had an extremely idealistic view of what a seminar should be: co-operative above all; exciting; and with everyone contributing and learning. More concretely, I wanted as complete a contrast as possible with the excruciating ninety-minute torture sessions I remembered sitting through as an undergraduate. Anyone with a degree has a ready-made source of good and bad practices, of what it's like to be on the receiving end: this turns out to be indispensable when you're first starting to teach.

I continued to try to provide broadly the same kind of seminar. But I soon realised that, for a large group of people of differing backgrounds, this may be more or less difficult; and so a range of different approaches and methods may be necessary. Never be afraid to try out new ideas and methods. Students will generally do what you ask them, if only because they think you are 'in charge'. Telling them clearly what you need them to do, and why, is important. A seminar is supposed to be a collaborative exercise. When starting with a new first-year group for the second time, for example, I asked them what they thought a seminar was, what it was for, and how they could contribute to and gain from it. Their ideas were very similar to mine - that they could learn from each other, express their own ideas, and so forth. And I think that this, for a while at any rate, effectively implicated them directly in responsibility for their own seminars.

Though it may contradict what I've said so far about students' expectations of you, relaxing and relinquishing control is probably one of the main things you've got to do. And this honestly doesn't take as long as you might think. After a few seminars I felt like I'd been doing it all of my life. In the very first one I found out how much the group knew about the subject matter of the course - little or nothing, as it turned out. Thereafter I knew that the unpleasant scenario of the students knowing more than I did wasn't going to arise. In fact, it never has: happily I can't tell you how to cope if you're faced with a room full of experts in your subject!

Timing is another vital practical consideration and is slightly more difficult to judge. At first I tended to gallop madly through topics, or linger to the point of tedium on one area, always trying to push the students further than they could or would go. The first seminar where teaching really started was unfortunately one of the most difficult, covering completely unfamiliar material that was quite complex. I prepared it well, and felt that here I had a stimulating, engaging seminar - and yet, disappointingly, it didn't go all that well. I just couldn't see what else I could do. But now I see that I was just cramming too much in. I wasn't giving people enough time to get to grips with the material. Again, I ought to have recognised this from my own experience, sitting through whole courses of seminars not understanding a thing. Because I had all this (I thought) tremendously _interesting_ stuff, I was determined to get through it all and to convince all of my students that it <u>was</u> tremendously interesting. Ideally, the group would probably take responsibility for staying on a topic until they feel happy with it. But until you and they are both ready for this, it's best to have a lot of reserve topics you can switch to. By all means overprepare: but don't let this encourage you to cram more into a seminar than will properly fit.

I suppose the moral of the story, therefore, is simply to have the courage of your convictions. Seminars can be great fun and rewarding. With any luck, your students will learn something. But if you make it apparent that you're prepared to let them descend into mini-lectures, then that is exactly what they will become.

Key points:

1   **Don't let nerves push you into being too rigid or into doing all the work.**

2   **Use your undergraduate experience of seminars, good and bad.**

3   **Try and use a range of learning methods which take into account the range of your students.**

4   **Use the physical environment to encourage or even force your students into more active responsibility for their own learning.**

5   **'Ice breakers' really are a good idea, honestly!**

6   **Let students dictate the pace; don't pack too much in.**

Lectures versus seminars: getting to grips with teaching

Gwilym Games

In my first year of teaching I did a limited amount of lecturing and a substantial amount of seminar work. My experiences in both of these areas certainly made me realise the significant difference in teaching style that they each require. From what I have experienced, I also suspect that the personal qualities required for successful lecturing may be far removed from those needed for successful seminar leadership. My experience also made me aware of the need for a careful analysis of the way I related to those I taught.

Lecturing

Since, for better or worse, I am blessed with quite a spirited personality, I wasn't actually that worried by the prospect of lecturing. Many people who I know 'freeze' at the prospect of talking before a large group. But it didn't really worry me. Constructing the shape of a lecture also proved quite fascinating as I was attempting to create something that was both informative and entertaining. All too well I remembered the sensation of listening to lectures which were either bland renditions of facts or contained no detail at all. Bearing in mind how inefficient lectures are increasingly acknowledged to be in merely imparting information, I decided to put most factual material in the handouts, using the oral presentation to draw a wider, and, I hoped, more evocative picture of what the implications of those facts were. This of course entailed considerable amounts of preparatory work. But it <u>was</u> intellectually satisfying because it forced me really to think very hard about a large number of separate areas and to gather them together into a coherent whole.

The actual delivery of the lecture seemed to go very well. People I talked to afterwards seemed quite satisfied by it and I was quite pleased. It certainly became apparent to me that lecturing is in many respects an extremely satisfying activity, combining elements of practical performance with genuine intellectual interest. On the other hand, thinking about it carefully also revealed its seductive dangers. Lecturing creates an intrinsically hierarchical relationship. A single person delivers the information and analysis, with everyone else excluded from participation. One only has to think of similar processes (like sermons, and, of course, speeches at mass rallies) in order to appreciate the problems inherent in the lecture format.

Seminars

These feelings about lectures were reinforced by my experiences in seminar teaching. Whereas lectures are quite simple and straightforward in structure, one orating to the many, seminars are meant to be a plurality, an open forum for the exchange of views and for debate between all participants. Even so, as many seminars illustrate, this is not necessarily the case in reality.

In general I found a real problem in ensuring that everyone contributed and that there were no awkward silences. If there were significant pauses, it became apparent that everyone expected me to fill in the gaps. Mature students, I found, were often a real blessing in such situations. They were not afraid of speaking out. All in all, though, I couldn't help comparing the stilted and stunted progress of a seminar with the type of debate and conversation one has in everyday life. It was such an artificial atmosphere - with heavy overtones of the schoolroom - that I wasn't really all that surprised that people had so little to say. From talking to other seminar tutors, I soon realised that these were common problems, though others were also having different ones. For some people, less forthright than I am accustomed to be, guiding seminar discussions was actually far easier than it was for me. But they in turn had greater problems with certain students dominating the discussions. My extrovert personality actually proved more of a hindrance than an asset in this type of teaching, resulting in my having too much of a dominating influence. It was in fact too easy for students simply to fade into the background rather than to contribute. It was quite an effort for me to adjust, and to learn to handle the situation.

I realised that, because seminars need multiple participation, you cannot control the outcome in the same way as you can structuring a lecture - no matter how much you prepare for them. All you can do is attempt to create the right atmosphere by choosing interesting activities and hoping that it turns out for the best. Each seminar group is different. What might work for one perhaps won't work for another. This means that you <u>must</u> be able to think quickly and to develop strategies for encouraging participation. Another factor was that, since I was teaching first years (students who had no experience either of the university environment or of the subject), what became apparent was that I needed to lower my expectations for the contributions that came out in seminars. I gradually realised that I must at first encourage virtually <u>any</u> attempt to contribute, no matter how banal or misguided it seemed. I needed systematically to attempt to build up self-confidence among the participants. When I <u>did</u> have criticisms to make, I realised that it was far better to do it in a gentle manner (something I found it difficult to bear in mind all of the time). It also occurred to me after a while that, rather than always trying to direct seminar discussions into particular areas, it was interesting to let the students find their own level at least some of the time.

In an effort to encourage better group discussions, I also experimented with different methods of teaching. I gave out a selection of primary documents for discussion. In doing this I discovered that the most effective method was assigning documents to specific people. Then in the seminar I was able to ask specific people to discuss their document and answer questions on it, a good way of encouraging more reticent individuals to contribute. I also experimented with debates - which, though highly effective with a motivated group, can be a disaster in other situations. Any type of activity which encourages people to break out of the rut of the standard seminar format is, I now feel, a step in the right direction.

All in all, my first year of seminar experience was not entirely satisfying. I noticed that my seminars were usually well attended, particularly when compared with those of some other tutors. But I felt that that was more to do with my 'gift of the gab' than their academic achievement. The students had probably found my seminars entertaining. Yet I was far from convinced that they really encouraged the oral debating skills they were supposed to. I suspect that successful seminar teaching is far from being a simple task. It probably takes a good deal of experience to know exactly how to handle certain situations and how to get things to flow smoothly. As a new teacher, you are in a learning process just as much as are your students.

Marking

As part of my seminar duties I was also expected to handle essay marking, an important activity on which it is worth adding a few remarks. I had thought that it would be quite difficult to simply give out marks to pieces of writing. But it soon became apparent that it was rather easier than it seemed. Luckily the course I was teaching on had clear guidelines for marking. These guided me in what to look out for. One thing I did find was that the impression I got when I read the first few pages of the essay usually tallied quite closely with the final mark I awarded. Compared to the actual teaching I found the marking relatively straightforward: even when you were eager to see that the mark did the work justice, it was invariably just a matter of spending time considering it.

On the positive side, marking gives you the luxury of time to reflect. (In the pressured situation of a seminar it is not always easy to say or do the right thing.) When marking you can consider carefully which comment to make on a student's essay and also to try to offer helpful advice. Some essays were easy to comment on, either because they were full of mistakes to correct or because they were so good that they encouraged my active engagement with their arguments. I did find, though, that 'middle-of-the-road' essays were more difficult to comment on. I found myself repeating, if not the same phrases, then the same sort of advice. This wasn't perhaps surprising. People often tended to make similar mistakes, in that they either fell into using too much narrative or went to the other extreme and used too much argument and too little detail. To conclude: marking was very far from being as frustrating as a seminar (in which success often seems to be out of your hands). Indeed, in assessing their written work, I could feel that I was contributing very directly to a student's learning.

Final hints:

1   Remember in seminars that you have to prevent yourself moving from leading the discussion to dominating it. It isn't as easy as it sounds!

2   Preparation is the key to success in lectures and seminars. Just make sure that <u>you</u> don't dry up in the lecture; try to make sure that <u>they</u> don't dry up in the seminars.

3   Don't get discouraged. University teaching is an activity, like life in general, which is both enjoyable and frustrating at the same time. When things look bad, you should remember that good seminars, essays and lectures do exist. Everyone faces problems, even if they are not the same ones.

"Hello, are you still here ...?"

Kirsti Evans

This must be a familiar greeting to anyone who has just completed a PhD. It is one that is often uttered by someone who has taught at the institution for decades but thinks that students just pass through on their way to bigger and better things. I return the greeting with an enigmatic smile. *Yes, I am still here,* I muse. I did my BA here, and liked the 'island of learning'. I liked it so much that I stayed to do a doctorate. But why exactly am I still here? Approaching middle age, having exchanged a 'Mrs' to a 'Dr': is it not time now to return to the 'real world'?

Whilst I was a research student I had already been teaching in the department on a casual basis, as one often does, for a term or two. And, after attending a training course at Lancaster, I became a Teaching Assistant in my department. But as yet I had not seriously contemplated a 'real' job as an alternative to the security of student life. Until, that is, the application for a fixed-term six-month lecturing post at another institution had to be in the post tomorrow. I decided I just <u>had</u> to do something. <u>Now</u>. Fill it in. Think: the post sounds interesting. Think: read the departmental 'blurb'. Yes, I agree with their ethos.

An invitation to the interview drops through the letter box a week before Christmas. It's the end of term. I'm too tired; can't make it; CAN'T THINK! I resolve to write a letter of apology for missing the interview, regretting passing-by a good chance of a job. A phone call. Nobody has been appointed, but could I go to see them after New Year? A second chance ... but why did they give me such an early appointment? I am teaching the day before. The day of the interview dawns, with me at the airport on a stand-by ticket, ready to board the first plane. By lunch-time I have landed my first lecturing job, starting in two weeks' time. HELP! The university where I am to teach is very helpful indeed. I had stated my 'specialist' areas at the interview, and also that I did not want to compromise my research interests. These wishes were, surprisingly enough, respected.

My first day at work. It has taken six hours to drive here today. I have to find my office, find my B & B and teach in two hours' time. I go into 'overdrive', get through the first session and stagger into my accommodation at 10 pm. On the practical side, because the contract is only for six months I decide not to sell my house but to commute the 500 miles a week. The driving takes an absolute minimum of 4½ hours each way. My little car 'dies' on the motorway five weeks into the job.

I sit in the AA truck with a pile of essays which I was taking home to mark in my lap and grimly contemplate the sorry sight being towed behind. Is it all worth the effort, not to mention the extra expense? Yes it is. The essays in my lap are testimony that the effort is indeed worthwhile. My thoughts move on to reflecting upon the teaching as we slowly make our way homewards.

I teach three different groups; three different subjects. As with any groups, there are differences, both academically and inter-actively. The way in which a group 'gels' seems quite significant from the point of view of subsequent learning experiences. My favourite group is the first-year group because the students are so open to ideas and to learning. With this group I can put into practice the ideas learnt on the training course. "Create a safe environment", we were told, "and students will learn to contribute as part of a positive and active learning experience." I can see it happening in front of my eyes. Towards the end of term the students are asking for more discussions, more group work. They no longer seem to rely on the tutor to do all of the talking.

Other strategies are needed for the second and final year students to change some of their passive learning habits. I remember the training session where we discussed positive and negative learning experiences. Positive experiences were to do with the student actively participating in the learning; negative experiences were to do with passively sitting in the back of the class trying not to become the focus of the tutor's attention. I look at the class and see a mixture of both. I do not wish to perpetuate negative learning patterns; I see the need to get the students to participate. I delve into my strategy-bag. It is not fair if I do all the work so I must devise a scheme to involve the students. But pushing the point now will only lead to avoidance behaviour. I drop the subject of student presentations for the time being. My chance, however, comes at the end of term. I combine exam revision with a series of topics; I circulate a list of 'time slots' and ask the students to work in pairs or groups. The rationale is two-fold. First, everyone has to revise for the exam: so why not do some of the work in the class? Second, I appeal to all members of the group to 'do their bit' - that is, to co-operate. The class responds, but there is still a fair bit of anxiety. Again, I remember what we learnt on the course about manipulating the physical environment. So I go into the room early on the days of the presentations to arrange the chairs into a 'friendly' circle.

The memory of the last few sessions is of sitting in a circle, the students gradually relaxing into a lively discussion. There is a genuine sense of having ended on a positive note.

Five hints:

1   Do something (about a teaching job) - but not until <u>you</u> feel ready. People often have a need for 'space' after finishing their degree. I had stared at this particular application form for a couple of weeks, only to be suddenly galvanised into action at the last minute. Try to work out whether you are a methodical person or one who is best when faced with tight deadlines. Find out what your strengths are (mine is 'enthusiasm about the subject').

2   Try to identify your needs. Do you want a full-time permanent job or are you happy to try different things first before committing yourself? I decided that I wanted to try out different institutions, different locations. So I 'target' temporary jobs.

3   Try to identify whether you want to be a 'specialist' or a 'generalist'. Established universities often look for a specialist, whereas many of the newer universities and colleges prefer a generalist. I was required to teach three different subject areas; something which was acceptable in a temporary job but which I would not like in a permanent job. Be prepared to communicate your preferences: the institution can sometimes make allowances.

4   Be honest with your prospective employers. At its most basic this probably means that you should only apply if you are genuinely interested in the job. In my case

being honest meant communicating both my fears and hopes to the employer.

5   Be prepared to accept that the job may not come to you and that you may have to travel far and wide to work. This has advantages and disadvantages. I have 'selected' areas (or even countries) where I would like to live and work, as well as ones I don't want to go to. I like to be either in the capital city or in the middle of the country. Which brings me back to our 'island of learning' ...

"Hello, are you still here?" "Yes, just finished teaching in London for six months; back at Lancaster next term. Cheers."

The Postgraduate Philosopher

Martin Gough

As someone who is now in his fifth year of teaching Philosophy in higher education, I can perhaps offer some reassurance to those starting as teachers. Some of the worries about how generally to teach well <u>do</u> dispel in time. For example, I can now look back on my first tutorial seminar meetings with mirth rather than anxiety - even when I recall the looks of blank horror on the faces of my tutees when I walked in with what I presumed was a confident and reassuring smile to announce "Hello, I'm your Tutor!" for the first time.

The scenario of meeting a seminar group for the first time, I imagine, is not dissimilar in other disciplines. There remains the pedagogical problem, more acute in Philosophy (if not unique to it), of how to turn students into good philosophers by academic teaching. In some other disciplines the goal of obtaining the unique 'right' answer prevails - even if students must also develop the skills for obtaining that answer. In most areas of Philosophy, however, it is important that we present, in order to do justice to debates both current and historical, a multiplicity of appropriate answers to a problem, each with its own strengths and weaknesses. It is likewise important that we appear open to new solutions, even those generated by relatively untutored 'off-the-top-of-the-head' contributions to discussion forums. Many students quickly latch onto the purpose of philosophical discussion and writing. But, *a priori*, there <u>is</u> a conflict which will cause puzzlement and frustration in other students. This conflict, which is properly a concern for the tutor, is about how he or she is to remain an authoritative figure with respect to the subject matter whilst not pushing a particular line in relation to a specific problem. (I have to say that this has now ceased to worry me from the point of view of my own teaching practice, even though I recognise that the theoretical question remains.)

I wish, however, in the remainder of this discussion, to concentrate upon what it is actually like to be a postgraduate student engaged in teaching Philosophy (and possibly other subjects) in higher education in the 1990s. My contribution is in part autobiographical and obviously it is based upon first-hand knowledge. And I want to suggest that, whilst much has certainly been done to improve the lot of undergraduates in terms of the practice of teaching Philosophy, too little attention is still, in my view, being directed towards the situation of the postgraduates charged with delivering that teaching.

As with all postgraduate students, my priority over the last few years has been my own course of study, in this case at the University of Leeds. And both the institution and my department agree that my completion of that course takes precedence over other tasks. However, as with a growing number of British students pursuing research in the Humanities, I have not been supported over this period, since October 1991, by a State Studentship from the British Academy. Indeed, the trend of larger numbers applying for fewer awards is worsening: in 1994 some 4,700 applicants (of whom 1,650 had first class honours degrees) were chasing only 1,000 new awards. Many postgraduates therefore, like me, have to secure funding from a variety of other sources.

My department has in fact employed me on a Teaching Assistantship contract with a part-time salary in return for my carrying out teaching and administrative work. This arrangement also involved part-time registration for PhD study, albeit in my case only for the first two years. Many other departments around the country have been advertising similar openings in recent years. And it's important to realise that the Teaching Assistantship scheme is not just charity on behalf of institutions for penniless candidates. The demand for postgraduate Teaching Assistants has arisen chiefly because of the recent expansion in undergraduate student numbers. Indeed, my workload has approached that of a newly-appointed lecturer, in terms of time commitment at least. I was, after all, tutor and main point-of-contact with the department for a large number of their first-year students.

It may be appropriate for postgraduates to enjoy only low status as teachers in the department. We are new to the profession. We should obviously not expect a level of income approaching that of full-time staff. I regard myself as fortunate in having been awarded the position which I have attained and to have gained a rewarding experience in teaching. But I do have a serious complaint. And this is that the position of postgraduates studying and teaching in Philosophy departments, whether or not within formal Teaching Assistantship schemes, is, on the whole, badly managed. Postgraduates, for example, have little or no say in the allocation of teaching loads within a department. Given the financial incentives underlying the expansion of student numbers, it is all too tempting for institutions steadily to increase the amount of tutoring which postgraduates do - at the same pace as, if not more than, for their full-time staff.

The issue of corresponding remuneration (or lack of it) is one thing; and, I say, not even the main thing. Rather, too little effort is made by some universities to understand the disparate needs and activities of the postgraduate teacher, taking into account all the different jobs that they have to do and the impact of those burdens on the time available for their own studies. There is no doubt that this situation is a consequence of the Government's funding formulae and the declining unit of resource. But it is often compounded by universities deciding to invest scarce resources in the more expensive, but potentially more lucrative, subjects such as the sciences.

The Teaching Assistantship scheme certainly should be a significant improvement on the more *ad hoc* hourly-paid arrangements for most postgraduate teachers, particularly when it comes to managing the relations between research, teaching and administration carried out by an individual. But too often departments are reluctant to commit themselves to guaranteeing the award of a Teaching Assistantship to an individual for the length of time required to complete a PhD part-time (presumably because of the long-term financial implications). They prefer instead to offer them for much shorter periods of time. This practice alone does little to refute the common accusation that departments treat their postgraduates merely as a convenient supply of cheap labour. Surely departments across all disciplines need to take greater care not to overwork their research students for their own purposes? This is not only because postgraduates are there primarily to study. It is also because their relative inexperience, at such an early stage in their research and teaching career, makes them especially vulnerable to diversion and, effectively, to exploitation.

In my view, the institutional background is, then, ultimately to blame for the failings of the Teaching Assistantship scheme, particularly in its operation in individual cases. My own university, at Leeds, has been embroiled in discussions aimed at setting standards for departments on employment conditions for postgraduates generally, following prompting by the postgraduate community both locally and nationally. I believe, however, that a bolder lead in directing the structure of postgraduate research should be taken by the body which holds the purse-strings for postgraduate study in the Humanities, namely the British Academy. The principal reason for this is that the postgraduate phase of one's career is meant to serve as training for a 'proper' academic job, the PhD being essentially a training qualification. The PhD is, of course, mainly a preparation for a research career. Yet the greater part of the working life of an academic in Philosophy (as in most other subjects) is eventually devoted to teaching. Surely properly-managed teaching experience at graduate level would provide better training for the future academic, with or without a formal qualification being awarded for this training?

Key points:

1 **There should be better managed integration of research and teaching at the postgraduate stage, including adequate financial support and more flexibility to suit individual needs as regards deadlines for research dissertation submissions.**

2 **The British Academy should introduce, in collaboration with departments, a new standard scheme of financial support for postgraduate research in the Humanities, in the form of the Teaching Assistantship with part-time registration for study.**

3 **In the event of being given the opportunity to teach, whether you are supported by an institutional Teaching Assistantship or you are to be paid an hourly rate just for the work you do, secure a written specification of all of your duties, to include both rates**

of pay for each specified task and the total number of hours you are expected to be spending on activities related to the tasks.

4   Do not be afraid to make clear your views to your department if you think that your workload is too much or that your work deserves more pay: liaise with your postgraduate colleagues to enable your department to obtain a representative picture of the situation and your recommendations for improving it.

How to make boring material interesting

Mike Bramley

Introduction

Let's get straight to the point. Statistics is boring. It involves numbers for one thing; and, for another, it involves doing things with complicated formulae. And who needs statistics anyway? Why should we have to tolerate the sheer boredom of standard deviations, means, medians and modes when we can leave it to calculators and computers? Anyway, why can't we just say *average*? Who's really bothered about levels of significance in the real world? What does it actually tell us? Statistics is just simply too abstract to mean anything to anyone!

Of course, let's not get too carried away. Statistics can be interesting, useful, and can say things about your data that qualitative analyses can not. Besides, there are occasions in which, no matter how hard you try, you simply have to engage in some sort of quantitative analysis.

Mention the word 'statistics' to undergraduates (I did!) and they may well recall feelings of fear and memories of psychotic maths teachers. There may be a fear of reliving those experiences, a frustration at not understanding, at being submerged in a mist of abstract formulae that means absolutely nothing. Or maybe the fear will come from some inherent effect that the word 'statistics' has - you utter the word and it's almost as if a semantic missile has obliterated all confidence.

statistics. They made comments largely to the effect of my first paragraph. I thought that I was ready for this, armed with several one-liners to the effect of those in my second. However, what I was not ready for, and, given thirty years, probably would still not be ready for, was being faced with a group of unsure, worried students. No one had warned me that students have feelings. All I knew was that my brief was to deliver seminar workshops on statistics.

In this essay I want to provide an account of my experience of teaching statistics to undergraduates, which was also my first teaching experience. I also want to discuss a few of the teaching strategies that I explored in this process. My intentions in doing so are not, of course, to prescribe a methodology to follow, but rather to explain what worked for me and, it seemed, for the students I worked with.

Background

The Course Module

Early in their second year all undergraduates within the linguistics degree scheme undertook a compulsory module entitled: Linguistics: Theory and Practice. The 'Theory' covered just that, whilst the 'Practice' involved quantitative techniques for the analysis of language. The statistical element of this module was assessed by a project which involved the selection and quantitative analysis of linguistic data.

The content of the module covered both descriptive and inferential statistical techniques, and both parametric and non-parametric tests of significance. All students were required to attend a lecture given by another member of staff, followed by a seminar workshop. I took four workshops, which comprised a total of just under one hundred students.

The Students

Three of the workshops consisted entirely of second-year students, whilst the fourth group was made up of both second-year BA(Hons) students and third-year trainee teachers. All of the groups also contained a mixture of mature students and school leavers, and the range of statistical experience was in all cases limited to GCSE or equivalent Maths courses.

Teaching Statistics

A preliminary small group exercise

One potential pitfall that I found in teaching statistics was that it is all too easy to assume that mathematical literacy and ability is roughly the same for all students. Assuming, however, is a dangerous game to play, and I soon realised that my seminar workshop groups were of decidedly mixed ability.

A further issue, which I had no idea was an issue before I started teaching, was how the students would feel about *doing* statistics. But how do you find out how students feel about statistics, and how can you get them to tell you without feeling too threatened or exposed?

A simple small group exercise, where groups of three discuss their experiences of statistics and then report back to the wider group with a list of feelings or comments, pays real dividends. Firstly, I found that it was a good ice-breaker. Secondly, it provides a less threatening environment in which group members can share their feelings and experiences of statistics.

Reporting back to the wider group makes all comments anonymous, so no-one should feel threatened or exposed. It also allows the whole group and the tutor to get a really good insight into the multiplicity of feelings and attitudes towards the subject being studied.

The feedback from this preliminary small group exercise was, in fact, very positive. One recurrent theme was that many group members were relieved to find that they were not alone in their qualms about *doing* statistics. One important point to note is that this exercise is not an attempt to stimulate a barrage of negative comments or feelings. Indeed the widespread feeling of relief was both based on students' discovering that other group members were apprehensive about statistics and also on hearing that there were others who were looking forward to studying statistics. In many respects, then, this is a useful preliminary exercise. It not only gives the group members an opportunity to share feelings and experiences. It also gives you an insight into the range of experiences and attitudes within the group, which may be useful for pitching the content of seminars or small workshop groups at your audience.

Dealing with the abstract

Statistics is in some important senses inherently abstract, and I found that, within all groups, some members were more able to grasp abstract concepts than others. Turning this on its head, one measure for helping students to begin to understand statistical techniques is to demonstrate that those techniques function in such a way as to break down abstractness. In this way, the functionality and purpose of statistical techniques is highlighted. For example, getting group members to call out their shoe sizes, or a numerical value which is not associated with anything which might make someone feel uncomfortable, is a good way of collecting data fairly quickly in the first session. This simple exercise also demonstrates an important point, namely that a collection of shoe sizes, or any other series of values, doesn't really mean too much as a list of numbers. In this sense it is abstract. However, what can be illustrated by this participative strategy is the usefulness of statistical techniques for breaking through such abstraction and for getting the data to tell us rather more about the shoe sizes of the group members.

Basic features of the data that could be highlighted here are, of course, the smallest, largest, most frequently occurring, and so on. However, at this stage the data can only show us so much. A graphical representation, a useful form of statistical technique, will show us much more. By developing this step-wise, progressive approach to the functionality of statistical methods and procedures, and by using them on real data, the inherent abstraction can be broken down to some extent. Of course, this is no sure way of ensuring that all students in a group are able to get beyond the problematical abstractness of the statistical. But I have found that this approach does help.

Using data

One further factor which might help group members begin to grasp the abstract is actually the choice of data used in exploring the functionality of statistical techniques.

Data must be relevant. Collecting shoe sizes may work for an initial exercise. But the applied nature of statistics means that group members have to be able to make links between the procedures and techniques which are explored in seminar workshop sessions and the potential uses of these procedures and techniques in their own work. The provision of relevant data is an essential conjunct in this learning process: the more varied the better. Obviously it would be impossible to collect data of relevance to the interests of every group member. But a broad range of data will at least show the potential of statistical analysis and go some way towards demonstrating potential areas of study.

I have, incidentally, found it helpful to accumulate sets of data well before the seminar workshop sessions begin: preparation is vital. Although this may not always be possible, a quick scan of discipline-related journals may yield a fair amount of data. If your own research (present or past) offers appropriate data, then this is another potential source. Either way, you should end up with a sizeable resource base which you can draw upon and utilise in future sessions.

Working with data in seminar/workshop sessions

One thing I have found fairly difficult is integrating statistics in a seminar workshop session in a way that is both interesting and interactive. It is easy, not least through nerves and inexperience, to fall into the trap of standing in front of a group, chalk in hand, going through examples on the board. This is something I did in the first few weeks of teaching. However, the students soon got bored and I realised that I needed to change my teaching strategy. It is always beneficial to reflect on your teaching strategy, and it is always useful to get feedback from group members. This need not be a formal feedback session; but talking to a few group members after a session can often provide invaluable pointers.

The teaching strategy that I adopted could be described as making the sessions more 'student-centred'. This is in no way a universal solution, or proposed as a prescriptive method for teaching statistics. But it worked well for the groups I taught. I created several different exercises for each session, using different sets of relevant, real data. Working in groups of three or four, group members worked through exercises. This gave group members who made mistakes the chance to work answers out together; and, if certain mistakes were common throughout the small groups, they could be addressed at the end of the workshop session in a plenary format. Furthermore, these exercise-based sessions extended as both my confidence in what I was doing and the students' confidence in what they were doing grew. This led, in the latter stages, to the introduction of small group presentations.

Of all the teaching strategies that I explored, the small group presentations were, in fact, the most successful. The strategy here was to supply each small group with either the same set of data and different tasks (in which case a full investigation of the data could be undertaken), or to give each small group a different set of data and the same task. Each group of students then worked through the data and was given a 5-minute slot at the end of each session to report back to the wider group on their mini-project, the techniques they used, and what they found. One point which needs noting here is that such a teaching strategy is obviously dependent on the group members having certain skills. And yet these exercises can be tailored for the skills-base of the group at a specific point in the course.

One last strategy which worked well in my first sessions was to provide data that was complementary: for example, an investigation of different features of child language at various stages in a child's development, or an investigation into specific stylistic features of written texts across different genres, and so forth. At the end of the sessions, you are able to bring each presentation into the plenary arena and draw wider conclusions from the work that the students have done in the session. Not only does this provide a real purpose for the small group presentations, it makes the sessions interactive, challenging, hopefully enjoyable, and likely to give students ideas of use in their own work.

Conclusions

I have recorded my experiences, and the strategies that I adopted in first teaching statistics, in the hope that those less experienced, and perhaps even those <u>with</u> some experience, may find something of use. I hope that you might in some way wish to draw upon them, and wish you well as you try to find what works both for you and your students.

Key points:

1   Never assume homogeneity in the ability of your group. Try to remember that they are all bringing with them a multiplicity of differing experiences.

2   Getting the group members to talk about their experiences in small groups could be a good ice-breaker, and may provide you with essential information about their attitudes and concerns towards the subject in a non-threatening manner.

3   Try to use a wide variety of relevant data. By doing so you are continuously making the connection between an investigative tool of analysis and the purpose for employing such techniques in breaking down the abstract.

4   If students are working in small groups spend time with all groups and bring common or recurrent problems/issues into a plenary forum for further discussion.

5   Keep reflecting on your teaching strategies, and where appropriate, try and get some informal feedback from a few group members.

The Junior Lecturer

Dominic Janes

Far from home, and far also from my old university, I have taken up a junior lectureship. In the light of the intensely competitive job market, it may seem petty now to wonder about questions of job title and status. After all, before your appointment, you may well have been staring at a long period of unemployment. Somehow, however, that eventuality has not come about. You have obtained the position of lecturer (fixed-term), in my case having been appointed for one year (or eleven months, it turned out, on reading the small print of the contract). But a job! A full-time job! One moment I was a hard-pressed PhD student. The next I have to consider my tax levels, get together a pension plan and face the fact that I am the youngest person in the department by a quantity of years it is wise not to calculate. I have gone from being one of them (students) to one of us (staff). Or should that be the other way round?

I am the same age as quite a few of the students (that is, 24 and ¾, if you must know). Indeed, I am far younger than many of those who my institution likes to describe as 'mature students'. But, even though my Young Person's Railcard has yet to expire, I am a student no longer. And the students themselves know this very well. I am no longer one of the mob. The staff, by contrast, are very friendly and welcoming. My arrival is a sign that their tribe is not, despite the Thatcher years, facing extinction. However, and this is just to point out a fact, most of the staff members have comfortable domestic lives in The Old Vicarage, Rustickthwaite, and the Mrs (almost all staff are men) and a cat and a potato patch for all I know, and they have no recreational reason to hang around in the department after the last batch of students of the day has slunk off from Reformation Studies. Do I have a slight feeling of not quite fitting into one group or the other?

So what am I saying? I suppose I am trying to make the point that the new appointee, fresh from doctoral glory (irony intended, of course), is likely to turn up, sign his or her tax and pension forms and settle down into, well, a sort of limbo. I keep wondering whether I am carrying the lecturer thing off properly. Are elbow pads and corduroy trousers items that can only be claimed with just a few more year seniority, when a beard would no longer seem premature? But just at the moment, my first pay cheque having just gone through the bank, I still have the same clothes, bag, glasses, and general paraphernalia of the postgraduate.

After one seminar, during which I had made a few ritual (but not *entirely* ritual) professions of lack of expertise as a new staff member, one student came up to me and said, "are you a real lecturer then, or what?" I could have drawn myself up, thought of England (as she was before the war, at least) and put the young man right. Of course I was a real lecturer and full lecturer! After all, was I not paid on the Lecturer A scale? We all know that money maketh man (and woman) in the 1990s. On the other hand, am I <u>really</u> a proper lecturer? After all, I am here mostly to mop up excess teaching that cannot be handled by existing staff. I am not in charge of any of the 'modules' I am teaching, and I have not chosen the course books, much less designed the courses. My job, perhaps, is to watch those to whom I am giving assistance, to learn their habits and personal peculiarities, and to reproduce them so as to produce a sort of 'virtual' Dr X or Professor Y; and so allowing him to virtually supervise two different seminars in two different rooms at the same time.

So, fluttering from one group of excess students to another, I have a strong feeling of living a sort of academic half-life, of being a stop-gap solution, of being like an insect that could at any moment be swatted, because, after all, mine is a (very) temporary appointment. My life, as far as this department is concerned, shall be a short one. Almost before I got here my thoughts and application letters were turning towards the planning of life after death; that is, the job after this one. On the other hand, such transient life-forms, suddenly flourishing and conveniently disposable, are no longer so much on the periphery of academic affairs. Departments, faculties, and 'study clusters', all are becoming increasingly dependent on what might be termed 'occasional labour'. The work of graduate supervisors, themselves keen to receive a little beef to add to the financial gruel-ration doled out by research councils, is becoming ever more important to departments in providing teaching in groups of a size that will still fit into seminar rooms built in the glory days of the sixties. The expansion of modular courses and the concept of subject flexibility and student choice will surely have major repercussions, not least in the form of unexpected fluctuations in student numbers. So, in future, there will probably be more 'junior lecturers' rather than less. The temporary lectureship may be an uncomfortable position to occupy. But at least some more 'bums' will have seats.

While I am on the subject of furniture ... I might just mention one last aspect of the junior lecturer's world: the bare and bleak office. My department is arranged around a long corridor. This is the public space and it is unloved, dressed in linoleum and swabbed down every morning by the cleaning staff. The rooms off it have, however, been turned by their long-term inmates into varied bowers of comfort. Sometimes a door will be left ajar and one will glance a plush sofa, or some monstrous pot-plant. From one room there sometimes emerges the sound of soft piano music (I presume from a radio or cassette-player). Another room gives off a strong whiff of gin and cigar smoke. My room, however, having been vacated, or rather, *stripped,* by its last occupant, is a space of echoing, blue-grey minimalist purity. White walls, two filing cabinets, a collection of chairs (ten, for seminars, none comfortable), and me: this faces the student eager for instruction on the grandeur that was Rome, or whatever it might be. No wonder they sit there grim and silent under the naked light-bulb as it swings gently from the ceiling.

But, just for the year, is it worth finding the money for a soft-furnishing make-over, for cushions, for a filter-coffee machine and a coffee table, let alone coffee-table books to go on it? No, the best must be made of the situation. My office is not so much *my* office as *an* office in which I am to work. It has probably only seen one occupant in the last twenty years and, in that perspective, I might as well be a student - no sooner arrived than ready to leave for other things. I recall that, when I first went to university, I spent the initial month carefully personalising my room, putting up posters just as I had them at home, and trying to make the place less strange, less foreign and intimidating. But now there is the great difference that this new university does not define my life in the way it does that of most of its students. Only if and when a permanent job comes along can I bring in the comfortable chairs and the pictures, and enjoy the luxury of being both a resident and an employee.

Little Time Out

Lou Armour

Since other essays in this collection have already advised that 'Prior Preparation and Planning Prevents Piss Poor Performance' I have no new practical advice to give. Subsequently, if there is a theme running through the vignettes below it is this: Teaching requires some instruction on 'How to' but no matter how good the advice, attending courses and reading 'How to' books is not 'teaching'. Sometimes the advice they give is rather banal. For example, books and stuff assert that each lecture and seminar is a different experience; but what of it? Who would expect otherwise? What formal instruction and advice seldom tell you is that what teaching is is of a myriad 'happenings' before, during and after any particular session.

Please make what you will of what follows.

Before: Sleepless in Lancaster

The night prior to supervising a mid-day seminar I attended a college dinner in my capacity as a college Assistant Dean and personal tutor to a number of the college's students. Needless to say, copious amounts of wine were consumed but I quietly congratulated myself on getting to bed by midnight and feeling only slightly tipsy. The next thing I remember is waking up and looking at my alarm clock - "Quarter to three: Jesus Christ!" I leapt out of bed praying that it was *a.m.* and not *p.m.* Drawing back the curtains, bright sunlight flooded into the room: "I'm dead!" I had missed the twelve o'clock seminar. I quickly decided what to do next: stay calm, shower, dress, go to the department and write to the class apologising for my absence ... with no excuses!

Whilst putting on my watch I noticed that although my alarm now stated 3.25 the time on my watch was 9.20. I remember thinking, "Which bloody one's correct?" Since both my watch and alarm run on batteries, I tried to figure out which contained the duff ones. Not having a second hand on either was a definite disadvantage. Naturally, I wanted to believe that my watch was in good working order but I also had to accept the possibility that I had slept in, even though I did not really believe it. I turned on the radio but that was no help. Eventually, I phoned a senior lecturer in the department: "I know this sounds stupid but what time is it?" "Twenty-five past nine." There is a God after all!

Members of staff rarely admit to having turned up late for seminars and lectures and yet we all know that it happens. The reasons for turning up late can vary of course; partying the night before, missing the bus onto campus, being ill (from the night before?), coping with a sick child, etc. Whatever the reason, you can bet your bottom dollar that the class will assume that if you are late then it is your fault. Indeed, when I told the class what had happened to me that morning one member of the class replied: "If I'm ever here and you're not I'll string you up by your nipples". A mature student and part-time nurse working nights who has to drive onto campus for a mid-day seminar can be most unforgiving!

Whether or not I have ever been late for seminars and lectures is by-the-by but no one ever told me that waking up could be a traumatic event. Maybe it's just me but a regular occurrence which happens upon waking is this: I'm never sure if I'm teaching that day or not; not because I don't have a diary (I do) but because the days seem to slide into one another. Consequently, on those days when I am not teaching, niggly little doubts that I am creep into my head. In other words: be prepared to awaken, think "It's Tuesday, no teaching" and then find your pulse increase as you think to yourself "Or is it Wednesday?" Even after establishing that it is indeed Tuesday, do not be surprised to find yourself wondering whether today is *inter alia* 'Office Hour', the day you've an early meeting with a particular student, the day to start marking and returning essays, and so on. If you're lucky enough to establish that it is safe to have a lie-in, don't worry: your pulse will return to normal just in time for your PhD to pop into your head. In other words, be prepared on your 'day off' to be unable to get back to sleep.

Sweet dreams ... Not!

During: Hale and Pace school of trendy advice

Play naming games with the class: 'Saddo' first years love it - "Hello Johnny" "Hello Billy" - but the saccharine-coated 'sandal-wearing-communal-caring-ness' of it all makes final year students want to puke. Wear a woolly jumper with your name on it if you wish to look like a prat (a tutor of mine once did) but leave the poor class out of it.

Try this: hand round a sheet of A4 for students to write their names on. Work out who 'X' is by noting that she is second from the right and thus second on the list ... (oh, how they'll laugh when you refer to the latecomer by the wrong name).

During: There are some things only a postgrad can do

Books and stuff say that theoretical ideas can be difficult to get across. Really? Wow! Help yourself by using a mixture of OHPs (without causing 'death by overhead'), 'real worldly' examples and recreations of some mundane activity with or for the class. The following is a good example of this.

The phenomenologist Alfred Schutz once observed that in order to get around the social world its members have to take a great deal of things for granted, and I thought that a good way of showing this fact would be by way of demonstrating the task I described as "following a recipe for scrambled egg on toast". I could have produced slides of cook book recipes and then asked the class what sorts of taken-for-granted knowledge each recipe instruction rested upon. I could have done that. But then, given the chance, why not actually follow the recipe quite literally and ask the class to write down the reasons why it all went 'wrong'? Done well, the advantage in demonstrating a theoretical point by practical exercise is that it reaches the parts overheads cannot; and, let's be honest, it also enhances your 'street cred'. The disadvantage is that you can end up reducing yourself and your lecture to a circus act whilst the class learns nothing.

I'd prepared everything beforehand and the students were extremely curious. What was underneath the towel? Why was the floor covered in newspaper? Why had Lou just walked in wearing full 'Chef's whites' and blue checked trousers? Ignoring the giggles and inquiring whispers I began the lecture as normal. Thirty minutes into the lecture Cath, a member of our support staff, casually strolled in with a handful of what looked like scrappy notes of some kind.

Pulling back the towel to reveal various items: a white box with 'TOASTER' written on it in black felt tip; a large metal bowl; a carton of milk; three eggs; a box of salt; three slices of bread and so on. I informed the class that I was about to make scrambled eggs on toast by following a set of instructions to the letter. Try it at home and you will see that, rather than ending up with scrambled eggs on toast, one ends up with an almighty mess: the toast ends up in flames, the egg-and-milk goes everywhere, and you're left looking like a Swedish chef out of *The Muppets*. In the classroom, on the other hand, the class are laughing and clapping; and, of course, you're loving it. It is then that you notice there is something different about the guy sitting at the front of the class. What is it? Oh, nothing a shower and a trip to the launderette couldn't fix.

Minor (?) problems aside, students tell me that they both enjoy the demonstration and get the theoretical point about so-called 'tacit' knowledge. That should please the 'books'. However, the real point of the story is neither to convince you that demonstrations are a good thing (you have to find that out for yourself) nor an attempt to sell myself as a 'hip' lecturer. No. The point of the story is simply this: a *full-time academic member of staff* does not have the 'street cred' to pull it off - but you do.

And After: Making use of others

Let's face it, the University, having accepted a student for entry, and the department, having passed a student from the first into subsequent years, is basically saying to you "This student is good enough to do your course". Well, as we all know, in the real world some students cannot be bothered to get out of bed in the morning and some are just plain 'thick' (at least this is what you will tell yourself sometimes). Nonetheless, it is quite natural to feel responsible in some way for both the successes and failures of one's students as a whole. For example, when I read a good essay I feel as proud as punch. And when I read a poor one I tend to feel a little disheartened. The personal ups and downs of essay marking are something I had to get used to; and so will you. Having said that, sometimes you will find that essays are neither good nor bad: just plain unreadable.

A very bright overseas student once handed me an essay on 'Organisations'. I knew from her seminar work and casual conversation that her spoken English was extremely poor; but then it was a damned sight better than my Chinese! Unfortunately, her written English was not so much poor as unintelligible. It wasn't her fault of course; after all, the University was no doubt very pleased with her fees. To be honest, I was a little annoyed that she had been put in the position in which she found herself and so I quickly made a mental note to mention this to the course convenor. Meanwhile, I faced the practical task of marking her work.

I spent hours on that essay. She knew what she was talking about, of that I was sure: the essay appeared to have a beginning, middle and end; the relevant terminology was in all the right places and correctly referenced and so forth. But it was simply impossible to read. After much worrying I decided privately to award the essay 67% and gave it to a senior member of staff to mark. He eventually deciphered it and thought it had the hallmarks of an Upper Second. I then informed him of my mark and the student's obvious intellectual abilities and we eventually decided to award the essay 65%. Come the exams we dropped a note to the external examiner requesting that he take a look at her coursework and exam scripts. I'm pleased to say that not only did she attain a First in the subject but her written and spoken English improved four hundred percent.

My Chinese is still non-existent.

A final word?

Books and stuff warn you not to take on too much. However, once you begin to feel like a departmental team player you <u>will</u> feel pressured to do more, either with your existing class or in terms of taking on extra teaching and marking; or even both. It's up to you what you do. But whatever you do, learn to say "No".

Key points:

1   You wouldn't believe who I've managed to get to call me if I haven't arrived by such and such a time.

2   Learn names by using them often. Simple.

3   Come on! You know what you hated about lectures so 'nuff said.

4   Here's a <u>slogan</u>: "There are no bad students only bad tutors". An admirable sentiment with an element of truth I suppose, but don't crucify yourself with it.

5   You're going to have a great time, but please don't jeopardise your thesis.

Further reading

Brookfield, S (1990) *The skilful teacher*, Jossey Bass Higher Education Series

Brown, S and Knight, P (1994) *Assessing Learners in Higher Education*, London: Routledge

Gibbs, G (1992) *Improving the Quality of Student Learning*, Bristol: Technical and Educational Services Ltd

Gibbs, G and Habeshaw, T (1993) *Preparing to Teach: an introduction to effective teaching in higher education*, Bristol: Technical and Educational Services Ltd

Laurillard, Diana (1993) *Re-thinking University Teaching: framework for the effective use of educational technology*, London: Routledge

Race, P (1993) *500 Tips for Tutors*, London: Kogan Page

Reynolds, M (1994) *Groupwork in Education and Training: Ideas in Practice*, London: Kogan Page

New Approaches to University Teaching

(A 15-day intensive course for new university teachers)

Lancaster is one of the universities with a high proportion of excellence ratings for teaching quality. Drawing on our experience and initiatives sponsored by the Unit for Innovation in Higher Education we offer a comprehensive course for new lecturers, postgraduate tutors, teaching assistants and anyone planning an academic career.

This course aims to introduce those new to teaching to theories of learning as they relate to teaching adults and to the practice of teaching in higher education. Using the video studio to record and practice a range of skills, participants will be able to develop and gain confidence in their abilities as teachers. As the title suggests there is a focus on new or innovative ideas in teaching, but traditional techniques are also covered.

A unique feature of the course is that we broaden the training from all aspects of teaching to all of the other roles a new teacher is expected to play. For example: course design and getting courses approved by faculty and Senate in your particular institutions, managing your own role in the sometimes adversarial environment of university departments and faculties, and making time for research.

The course has a structured programme to lead participants through the minefield of difficult situations and we will look at worst case scenarios like student appeals and dealing with harassment. However, the overarching theme is the development of confidence and the ability to inspire students. Each participant will be encouraged to reflect on and develop

91

a personal teaching profile which plays to their strengths and offers advice and help on the things that need further work.

A sample of the areas to be covered:

- Traditional and interactive lecturing
- Tutoring in seminars, workshops, field trips and practicals
- Supervising dissertations and group projects
- Information technology - WWW, e-mail, conferencing and TLTP
- Special needs including dyslexia
- Academic counselling and managing the boundaries of your role
- Juggling teaching and research commitments
- HEFCE Teaching Quality Assessment simulation.

New Approaches is a complete course, suitable for those teaching in any discipline. It can be taken as an MA module, as part of a PhD training programme or as professional training.

For further information: Amanda Thompson, Conference Secretary, School of Independent Studies, Lonsdale College, Lancaster University LA1 4YN (Fax 01524 843934, telephone 01524 594474/593888 (24 hours) or Email: IndStud@lancaster.ac.uk).